I0152518

Nothing Can Stop You This Year

"**Amazing ways to get more done in less time!**"

Dr. JoAnn Dahlkoetter, author of *Your Performing Edge* & coach to Olympians

"**Uncovering the secrets of 'unstoppability,' Tom Marcoux is the shining light of get-it-done. I love this book.**"

David Barron, coauthor of *Power Persuasion* (www.Power-Persuasion.com)

Praise for Tom Marcoux's other work

"In *[Be Heard & Be Trusted]*, Tom teaches potent tools for finding your voice and powerfully expressing yourself, essential for getting what you want in life."

Marcia Wieder, author of *Making Your Dreams Come True* and PBS celebrity

"Tom's *How to Heal When Life's Too Much*, helps if you are having a rough time. I'd recommend it to clients, colleagues, and friends."

Shannon Seek, Principal, Seek Solutions, author of *Organic Organizing Matrix*

"In *Online Secrets to Build Your Brand*, Tom [gets you] more cash per click."

David Barron, persuasion expert, coauthor of *Power Persuasion*

"Tom's *How Top Salespeople Double Sales in Half the Time*, provides me with new techniques that I use."

Steven Seitz, Sales Manager, Silicon Valley Conference Center

"Hiring Tom Marcoux as my media and marketing coach was the most valuable thing I've done in several years."

Dr. JoAnn Dahlkoetter, author of *Your Performing Edge* & coach to Olympians

Nothing Can Stop You This Year!

*I help people experience enthusiasm, love,
and wisdom to fulfill big dreams.*

TOM MARCOUX

Personal Mission
Caption

OTHER TITLES BY

TOM MARCOUX

❖

Be Heard and Be Trusted

Wake Up Your Spirit to Prosperity!

Wake Up Your Spirit to Prosperity for Couples!

Secret Influence to Get You Out of Trouble

Online Secrets to Build Your Brand

Power Time Management

10 Best Kept Secrets of Persuasion Masters

Double Your Sales in Half the Time

Say Yes to Yourself

Personal Branding

How to Heal When Life's Too Much

Truth No One Will One Tell You:
How to Feed Your Soul, Save a Business, or Get a Job in a Crisis

Darkest Secrets of Persuasion and Seduction Masters:
How to Protect Yourself and Turn the Power to Good

Empower Your Personal Brand:
Align Yourself for Promotions and Raises

Nothing Can Stop You This Year!

How to Unleash
Your Hidden Power

to Persuade Well, Get More Done,

Gain Sudden Profits, Command Intuition,

& Feel Great

2nd Edition

❖

Tom Marcoux

America's Communication Coach

&

The Time-Leverage Detective

A QUICKBREAKTHROUGH EDITION

ISBN: 0-9800511-5-0 / 978-0-9800511-5-5

© 2010 Tom Marcoux Media, LLC

All rights reserved, including moral rights. No part of this book may be reproduced without written permission from the publisher.

QuickBreakthrough Publishing is an imprint of Tom Marcoux Media, LLC

More copies are available from the publisher:

Tom Marcoux Media, LLC
(415) 572-6609
TomSuperCoach@gmail.com
www.TomSuperCoach.com

This book was developed and written with care. Names and details were modified to respect privacy where necessary.

Interviews and substantial excerpts by other authors are copyrighted by those authors and included herein with their permission.

❦ This book was published using green technology. The inks used contain no substances listed as hazardous air pollutants per §112 of the Federal Clean Air Act and emit virtually no volatile organic compounds (VOCs), unlike traditional books.

Disclaimer: No fiduciary relationship is created hereby between the reader and author or publisher. The author and publisher note that each person's situation is unique and that readers have the responsibility to seek consultations with health, financial, spiritual, and legal professionals when implementing any advice contained herein. The author and publisher make no warranties of any kind, and shall not be liable for any special, consequential, or exemplary damages resulting, in whole or in part, from the reader's use of, or reliance upon, this material.

kunst+aventur

Book design, indexing, + photography by

see *Collophon* at rear

Dedication

*this book is dedicated to the
terrific book & film consultant*

JOHANNA MAC LEOD

Acknowledgements

My heartfelt gratitude to all my other team members. Thanks to the guest authors for their voices of great experience. Thanks to Linda L. Chappo, and to Sun Editing & Book Design (www.SunEditWrite.com) for editing. Thank you to Stacy Diane Horn for editing additional material for the expanded edition. Thanks for comments from my father, Al Marcoux. Thanks to my mother, Sumiyo Marcoux, a kind, generous soul. Thanks to Gregg at Kunst+Aventur for the book's cover, design, editing, fact checking, typesetting, indexing, and production logistics. Thanks to Higher Power, our readers, our clients, and our enthusiastic audiences.

Contents

Summary Contents

Detailed Contents

Contents

Part I

1

WHAT IS A BREAKTHROUGH FOR YOU?

2

BUILD THE CASTLE FIRST

3

ENERGIZE

4

SURROUND YOURSELF WITH THE COMPELLING

5
TURN AROUND YOUR MOODS

6
B.E.S.T. PRINCIPLES

Part II

7

QUICK BREAKTHROUGHS FOR YOUR SUCCESS

8

QUALIFY

9

USE TIME-LEVERAGE

10

INTUIT TO DO IT!

11
CREATE (DON'T COMPETE)

12
KINDLE BRAND

Part III

13

10 BEST KEPT SECRETS OF PERSUASION MASTERS

14

PREPARE

15

EMOTIONALIZE

16
REVEAL BENEFITS

17
SET UP SIMILARITIES AND PARTICIPATION

18
UNLEASH STORIES

19
ASK QUESTIONS

20
SHOW YOUR PERSONAL BRAND

21
INCREASE LISTENING

22
ORGANIZE PERSONALTAINMENT BRANDING™

23
NURTURE TRUST

Part IV

24

Secrets of Being Unstoppable

25

Nonresistance

26

Nonjudgment

27

NONATTACHMENT

Appendices

Part I

1

What is a Breakthrough for You?

I never expected to write *Nothing Can Stop You This Year*, but two things happened that shook me to the core.

First, one of my college students suddenly took ill and ended up in the hospital during finals week. It was his heart.

Second, I saw a young motorcyclist who had been hit on La Cienega Boulevard in Los Angeles. He was years younger than I, and I couldn't help but notice his blood mixing with gasoline in the gutter. He died, and my soul screamed, *I want to live!*

Seeing the death of the young motorcyclist prodded me to make big changes – I ended an eight-year relationship, I moved and I took leaps forward with my life work.

Why am I telling you this? Because before I saw the motorcyclist die, I had been in a trance. I had convinced myself that my life was good enough. It wasn't good enough. I had been stuck. I had been stopped. Can you relate to that?

I trust that you can. My student, who had difficulty with his heart, reminded me how fragile life is. That's why this book is for you – *Nothing Can Stop You This Year.*

Let's Talk About Your Breakthrough

You want something. What? More success? Fulfillment? Better relationships? If I asked you, "How are things going?" it is likely that you would mention something that you find to be an obstacle. You would likely complain about something being less than ideal. Let's face it together – you want a breakthrough. *We won't let anything stop you.* I will now be your coach. From this page forward, your better life begins.

You have in your hands a book filled with story after story of how people made big dreams come true. You'll learn how *10 billionaires and millionaires* applied principles that we will cover in this book, and how *nothing could stop them* from gaining lives of success and fulfillment!

Often, when I go on television and radio shows, I'm referred to as the "Time-Leverage Detective." For the callers, I do real-time detective work to help them leverage their time. I ask questions that you will find in the chapters of this book and that unfold practical answers.

You Will Learn How to Access Your Intuition

This book is about making breakthroughs to create *your best year* ever. Your intuition is an important part of the process of making breakthroughs. Your intuition can give you a real advantage. In the chapter *Intuit to Do It!* we cover *Secrets for Sudden Profits.*

When the time came to name this book, I recalled my father's favorite phrase in all our conversations, "Tom, nothing can stop you."

Since I had trained my intuition to give me powerful feelings of certainty, I realized that *nothing can stop you* was the ideal title and focus for this book.

Researchers have noted that many extremely successful people have credited their intuition, or "gut feelings," for having guided them to their best decisions.* We will explore powerful questions that you can pose to your intuition in order to gain valuable guidance.

Seeing the young motorcyclist die happened years ago, but the image is vivid to this day. From that moment, I made new choices and took new action. My intuition signaled that it was time to make big changes. *The results were beyond what I could have imagined* before that life-changing event. Bestselling author Og Mandino said that our lives are changed by the people we meet and the books we read. Please use this book as

....

* Dr. Gerd Gigerenzer, author of *Gut Feelings: The Intelligence of the Unconscious* is the director of the Max Planck Institute for Human Development in Berlin. His breakthrough studies are on the nature of intuitive thinking. "My research indicates that gut feelings are based on simple rules of thumb, what we psychologists term 'heuristics.' These take advantage of certain capacities of the brain that have come down to us through time, experience, and evolution. Gut instincts often rely on simple cues in the environment. In most situations, when people use their instincts, they are heeding these cues and ignoring other unnecessary information," Dr. Gigerenzer said, as noted in "Through Analysis, Gut Reaction Gains Credibility," Claudia Dreifus (*New York Times*, August 28, 2007).

your turning point. Your best life begins when you apply what you learn from this book.

Nothing Can Stop You If You Never Give Up*

What stops many people?

- Lack of money

- Lack of confidence and paralysis caused by fear

- Lack of time

- Lack of contacts

- Lack of strength

- Lack of energy

••••••••••••••••••••••••••••••••

*One of my editors said, "Some people unfortunately label as possible a dream that is truly impossible." My reply was that what concerned me was that the process of labeling is often done in the absence of information and time. For example, it broke my heart when I had a girlfriend who wanted to sing the lead part in the musical *The Phantom of the Opera*, but she was tone deaf. So I acknowledge that she held an impossible dream. But I admire that she continued to stay active in musical theater as a dancer. So I witnessed her modify her dream and still derive fulfillment. I'd also like to add that it often helps to devote extra effort to get training and feedback from a number of teachers, experts, or other learned people in the field that you want to excel in. So when I say "nothing can stop you if you don't give up" I mean that if your goal is to have a meaningful life and you have the flexibility to modify your dream like my former girlfriend, you can experience meaning and fulfillment. I want to encourage you to pause for a moment and take a good look to see whether you have made a hasty judgment that something you deeply desire is truly impossible. I personally know people who have started with no money and no contacts and then made a feature film that was distributed. I know people who have recovered from cancer. Please know that holding a personal vision and developing a supportive circle of friends, mentors, and family members is truly valuable.

- Lack of persuasion skills
- Lack of awareness of the Secrets for Sudden Profits
- Procrastination

You can get through these challenges when you use the secrets and proven methods of this book. A few paragraphs down, I identify particular chapters that address these challenges.

Using this book will strengthen you!

How? You'll learn to use the Secret of Real Power.*

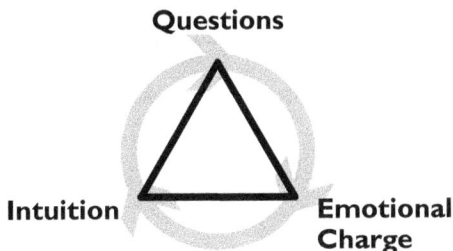

The Secret of Real Power

Questions

Intuition

Emotional Charge

Real Power Triangle

Every Chapter of This Book Includes Power Questions

Power Questions are your inroad to intuition. Through your intuition, you access a higher level of wisdom and knowledge.

• •

* As diagrammed, the trio of Questions, Emotional Charge, and Intuition are interdependent. Often, one cannot get to the Emotional Charge without effective Questions. Likewise, when examining one's thoughts and feelings inspired by Questions, one gains access to "hidden" Intuition.

How do you feel at this moment? When you read this question, did you suddenly check for discomfort in your body? That's my point! We have been conditioned to look for an answer immediately when we hear a question.

To get the most value from this book, I suggest that you purchase a journal or notebook to keep with your copy. Use it when you do the exercises and answer the Power Questions at the end of each chapter.

Just devote 20 seconds to writing your answers in your journal, and you can make a breakthrough! "Tom, I really appreciate your questions. I start looking at things in a fresh way, and I find my own solutions," my client, Maya, told me.

The questions plus your answers *give you an Emotional Charge.* This is a crucial element for improving your life. You can read a self-help book, nod your head, and think, "Yes, that's a good idea." But *the power flows* when you do a brief exercise. Doing the exercises for 20 seconds will benefit you more than reading for ten hours.

The questions and exercises in every chapter will enable you to attach emotion to a task or method. We won't play Pollyanna and hide from reality. We'll use what it takes to get positive results. If fear of tax penalties is the only thing that gets you to do your tax paperwork, we will incorporate that to make you strong and empower you to be *a happy achiever.* For example, in Part I, Chapter 2: *Build Your Castle First,* we will explore how to approach getting things done, while simultaneously reducing stress. That is part of being a happy achiever.

Let's face it – Emotion puts us into action. That's why we need to access emotion. We need to attach an Emotional Charge to what we want to do or change. Then, we take the action steps inspired by this book. That's when *Nothing Can Stop You!*

The Einstein Factor Secret

Albert Einstein said, "*You can never solve a problem on the level on which it was created.*" This means we need to rise to a higher level. I call this the *QuickBreakthrough Level.*

The *Einstein Factor Secret* propels us to learn to shift to the *QuickBreakthrough Level* of perceiving, feeling, thinking, and acting. Shifting to the empowered state of the QuickBreakthrough Level gives us heightened awareness and flexibility.

"That's a tall order. Not many people can do that," One audience member responded.

"Maybe not at this moment. But by just being human, each one of us has this potential," I replied. "I was talking with my friend, Dr. JoAnn Dahlkoetter,* who coaches CEOs and Olympic gold medalists … and we noticed how she 'gets into the zone' when she gives a speech. She can respond to any question. She says things that even surprise her in terms of how helpful they are."

That's what *Nothing Can Stop You This Year* is all about. You learn to function on the QuickBreakthrough Level. You get into the flow of:

- Intuition
- Cooperation
- Connection

....
* DrJoAnn.com.

- Creativity
- Integrity (wholeness)
- Excellent communication
- Effective action

On the QuickBreakthrough Level, you are free from distraction, pain, worry, limited thinking, judgments, and emotional baggage. You do *not* procrastinate. (See Part II, Chapter 9: *Use Time-Leverage.*)

Your hidden power is your ability to shift to the QuickBreakthrough Level. Another important secret:

Progress is not enough.
We want a Breakthrough.
We really want the feelings that
a Breakthrough brings.

So How Do We Shift to the Quick Breakthrough Level?

We shift to the QuickBreakthrough Level using any number of the techniques contained in this book. These include the TriggerSet Method, the Easethrough, the elements of persuasion, and the elements of the Q.U.I.C.K. Process. We will begin with the Easethrough.

The Easethrough Brings More Benefits than a Breakthrough

The idea of rising to the QuickBreakthrough Level includes what I call the *Easethrough*™, which is better than a standard breakthrough. A breakthrough implies that there is resistance that one must punch through. The idea of the *Easethrough* is to neutralize the resistance. You ease through! The *Easethrough* is further discussed in Part III, Chapter 13.

~~~~~~~~~~~~~

As I promised, I am showing you which chapters address particular problems. If a topic below grabs your attention, your heart, and intuition are inviting you to start there.

Where to Find Solutions

- **Lack of money.** To gain a job or clients, use a powerful personal brand. (Part II, Chapter 12: *Kindle Brand*)

- **Lack of confidence and paralysis caused by fear.** Learn what empowers you. (Part I, Chapter 2: *Build Your Castle First* and Part II, Chapter 9: *Use Time-Leverage*)

- **Lack of time.** (Part II, Chapter 9: *Use Time-Leverage*)

- **Lack of contacts.** (Part II, Chapter 12: *Kindle Brand* (Part 2), especially the section on listening.)

- **Lack of strength.** (Part I, Chapter 3: *Energize*)

- **Lack of energy.** (Part I, Chapter 3: *Energize*)

- **Lack of persuasion skills.** (Part II, Chapter 12: *Kindle Brand*)

- **Procrastination.** (Part II, Chapter 9: *Use Time-Leverage*)

- **Secrets for Sudden Profits.** (Part II, Chapter 10: *Intuit to Do It!*)

Like other books in my QuickBreakthrough series, this book is designed to be clear and concise.

A Bonus of this Book

In Part I, Chapter 3: *Energize*, you'll learn the secrets of losing weight. I prefer the words "Get lighter," because they are empowering.

~~~~~~~~~~

Are you wondering how your author has made breakthroughs and dreams come true? Over the years, my perspective has expanded as I enjoyed adventures that required money, contacts, and strategies. I am grateful for my experiences connected to prosperity including:

- Directing and producing feature films
- Travel to various parts of the world
- Speaking at the National Association of Broadcasters Conference (among the world's largest media conferences) six years in a row
- Teaching as a guest instructor at Stanford University
- Publishing my business books, music, and novels
- Taking fun vacations with my romantic partner and our parents

As I was the first college graduate in my family, I live with a lot of hope.

Let's increase the hope and joy you feel on a daily basis. You will learn, through this book, how to access your hidden power. You were born with hidden capabilities to access your intuition and even the intuition of other people (which is the reason I guide you to learn listening skills). When you take action, and use the proven methods in this book, you will take a leap forward towards realizing your big dreams.

The idea is for you to have the best year in your life so far.

Read on and start your best year! Now, let's dive deeper into the process for you to make a breakthrough.

What is a Breakthrough for You?

An audience member asked me, "A breakthrough in one year? Isn't that up to God or the universe? What about the actor who endures years before he lands the breakthrough role? How about the entrepreneur who only succeeds with her second company?"

"It's a matter of viewpoint, mindset, and action," I replied. Breakthroughs are needed all along the way. Each year, we have the potential to rise to a higher level. Let's view this process as a staircase. We can rise to Breakthrough 1 this year. That's Step 1. Next year, we can rise to Breakthrough 2. Perhaps at Step 3, a big, flashy breakthrough happens. But it only happens because we leapt to a new level in previous years."

The Breakthrough Staircase

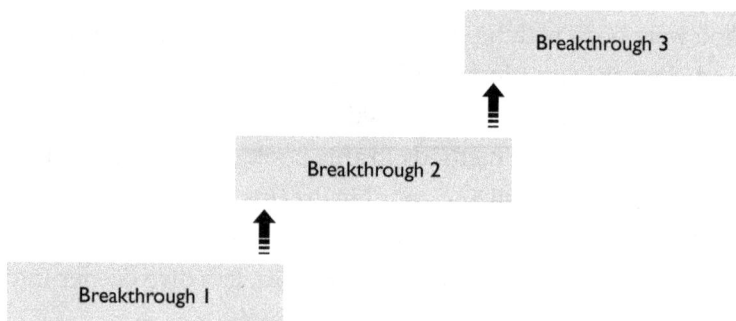

I continued, "But there's more to this. How do you feel now? How do you feel about this year? How do you feel about your life? I know that my lowest points in life were when I felt trapped and without hope. When you use my methods to live on, the

rendered by Chris Sehenuk

QuickBreakthrough Level, you feel it in your bones. You know you're making progress. *You feel hope!* You're living on a whole new, exciting level. You are proud of yourself. We're talking about breakthroughs in your thinking and action."

This book is about getting yourself to take action – to break through anything that binds you.

Years ago, actor Joe Pesci had given up on acting and was managing a restaurant when he received a phone call from Robert DeNiro! How did he get that call? Joe had performed in a small feature film, and Robert DeNiro had seen it. As a result, Joe gained his big, flashy breakthrough and appeared as Robert DeNiro's brother in *Raging Bull*, directed by Martin Scorsese. For an actor, a career is a series of breakthroughs – the first paying job, the first commercial, and the first role in a feature film.

Your Best Life is a Series of Breakthroughs

Later in this book, I share with you the *Milestones Binder* – you record the new actions that you take for the first time in this new year.

Many people do not know how to recognize a breakthrough. Let's take action now. Your first action is to take a guess as to what a breakthrough might look like in your life. In 20 seconds, write down an outcome that you really want to occur. Write this on the "Desired Outcome" level of the Breakthrough Staircase below. Then, on the steps below this, quickly write your first ideas about what breakthroughs would lead to your better life.

The Breakthrough Staircase

Breakthroughs take various forms. Some even have a spiritual element:

- Breakthrough in forgiveness
- Breakthrough in feeling "lighter" (relieved of a burden)
- Breakthrough in enjoying life each day

Now, fill in *your* answers:

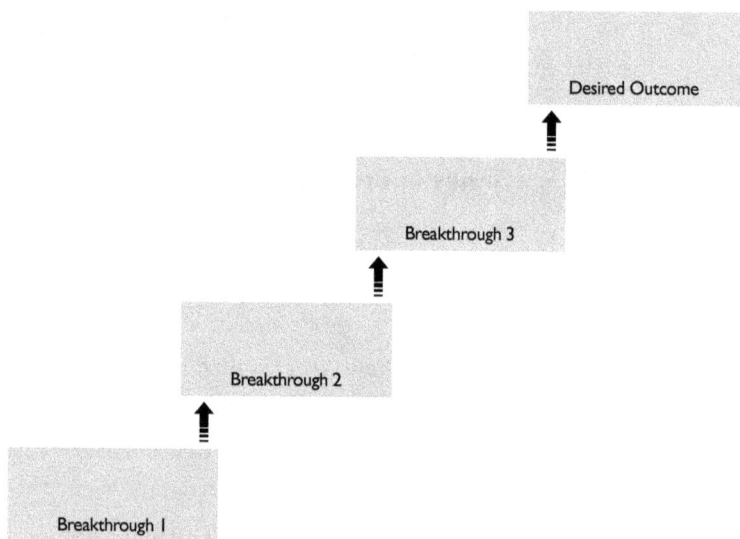

Let's Get Clear About Your Breakthrough

My clients have written that a breakthrough can do the following:

- Help me feel better
- Increase my income – a lot!
- Give me a job that I love
- Bring a terrific romantic partner into my life

The breakthrough will bring you benefits. In your journal, repeat the process above by writing a second version of your Breakthrough Staircase. See if your answers have changed in some way from what you wrote the first time.

The Real Power in the Breakthrough

While working with clients, I have found that the power in the breakthrough is related to *feelings*. My clients put more effort toward creating a breakthrough when they feel what the breakthrough will bring. Power lies in feeling a bit of what you really want and what you imagine the breakthrough will give you.

Process 1: Preview feelings that a breakthrough will bring

The truth is that we strive for a breakthrough because *we want to feel something*. When someone says, "I want a romantic partner," he or she wants to feel comfort, companionship, and the warmth of love. A person who says "I want to be successful" may want to feel strong and independent.

To continue looking at feelings, let's consider a dialogue I had with my client, Martha.

1. What do you want?

To be successful.

2. What do you want to feel?

I want to feel successful in my own business.

3. What will being successful do for you?

I won't have to worry about money and bills.

4. And then you will feel …?

Free! I won't feel this burden on my shoulders – the constant fear that I won't be able to provide for my daughter Mei to attend a good college.

5. When you can provide for Jimmy to attend a good college, you will feel …?

I'll feel like a good mother. I'll feel that the hole in my chest will fill up. I'll feel the full, warm feeling of knowing that I have truly expressed my love for Mei.

I call this process a preview of feelings that a breakthrough will bring. Now, it's your turn. In your journal, answer these questions.

1. What do you want?

2. What do you want to feel?

3. What will _____ do for you?

4. Then you will feel …?

5. Now, imagine that you've had the breakthrough. What are you feeling?

Good work!

Process 2: Preview of coming attractions – Feel it now!

In this process, you can experience some of the feelings that your breakthrough will bring. For example, my client, Tara, wants to star in feature films. She can feel some of the joy this week. How? She can borrow her brother's video camera to videotape a close-up of herself performing a monologue. She can play the videotape and watch herself acting on her television screen. This will be a preview of watching herself in a feature film on a DVD. Tara said, "Tom, that experience gave me a rush!" She felt thrilled.

Now it's your turn. In your journal, write down the answer to – How can you feel (on a simple level) part of what you will feel when your breakthrough occurs?

Process 3: Create a "commercial"

A number of my clients have found it helpful to create an audio or video commercial to activate their feelings and their subconscious mind. This process inspires the energy and persistence to bring on your breakthrough. For example, my clients, David and Sarah, created a video "commercial" together. Sarah operated the video camera while David introduced the video.

David started. "Welcome to our cruise vacation. [points to brochure photos.] Here is our ship. Now, look at this gorgeous sunset seen from the bow."

Then David filmed. Sarah said, "Here is the grand staircase that leads to the dining room. Oh! Look at these terrific desserts…. This is the gym where I can take aerobics classes. Then, I can eat and eat!"

After the video was completed, David and Sarah repeatedly played it in their bathroom while they brushed their teeth and prepared for work in the morning. They were energized to find new ways to expand their business so they could afford the cruise.

Another option is to make an audio commercial that you play in your car while commuting to work.

Now, it's time to go into action. Write details of your own commercial in your journal. Remember, this is a book for you *to do*, not just to read.

Easethrough Brings More Benefits than a Breakthrough

The idea of rising to the QuickBreakthrough Level includes what I call the *Easethrough*™, which is better than a standard breakthrough. A breakthrough implies that there is resistance that one must push through. With the *Easethrough*™, you neutralize any resistance. You truly ease through!

Picture someone who wants a breakthrough, so he does a karate chop and breaks a board. Now, with the *Easethrough*, you eliminate the board and just move forward. That's much easier.

Benefits of the Easethrough

- Save your energy
- Get the pain out
- Eliminate procrastination
- Have more fun
- Enjoy your daily life

We will explore the Easethrough™ in later chapters of this book.

Part II, Chapter 9: Time-Leverage – When you learn to get the pain out, you neutralize your own resistance. You eliminate procrastination. You get more done!

Part III, Chapter 13: 10 Best Kept Secrets of Persuasion Masters – Persuasion masters eliminate resistance in their listeners.

~~~~~~~~~~~~~~~~

This book is designed to enable you to make this year into *your best year ever*. In the next chapters, we will use the B.E.S.T. Process:

B – Build the Castle First

E – Energize

S – Surround Yourself with the Compelling

T – Turn Around Your Moods

We'll get your Best Year started in the next section.

2

Build the Castle First

Walt Disney said, "Build the castle first." Walt's intention was that his tough construction people would know that when they were building Disneyland, they were building something that had never existed before. Now, you are building something that has never existed before – your great year and your big dream.

Walt showed the construction crew that Disneyland was full of magic – as represented by the castle. Now, we're going to build your castle – your big dream.

Step 1: What Outcome Do You Want?

First, answer this question and write down your answer in your personal journal – *If the genie of Aladdin were next to you and you could have or do anything, what would that be?*

Write it down now – in the next 20 seconds.

Good! Let's get at it another way.

So the big dream is real in your life. What feels great about it? Write your answers now.

Well done! You're on a roll.

Step 2: Your Great Year Letter

Next, imagine that this best year of your life (so far) has turned out fabulous – better than you could have imagined it. Picture yourself writing to your friend about this amazing and enjoyable year. Now, on page 24, write *Your Great Year Letter.* Fill in the blanks. Do this quickly. Don't let your rational mind slow you down. You're in the toy store of the universe. You have a gift card with no charging limit. Wow! Don't stay in the "Okay, my life is good enough" trance (like the trance I had been in before I saw the death of the young motorcyclist).

This is your moment. You deserve a better life. This better life is in your hands now. On page 24, fill in the blanks right now.

Yes! Well done. Now make a copy of the form. Put it in your purse or day planner. Make another copy and place it on your bathroom mirror. You need to see this letter daily.

You probably noticed that many details of Your Great Year Letter emphasize feeling great. This will enable you to increase your productivity and feelings of fulfillment, whether or not you are a *for-the-team person.*

Are You a For-the-Team Person?

I say "for-the-team," because many of us will do more for family members or friends than for ourselves. If you're this kind of person, you may have found that setting traditional goals for your personal enrichment has not worked. If you set goals that enrich your life plus your family's life, you will find your hidden power in those goals.

For example, my client, Serena, discovered that she pressed forward in making a Web site when she made the decision that 20% of each sale would go toward her daughter's college education. She set up a separate account where she put aside that special 20%.

If you are a for-the-team person, be sure to write this part of Your Great Year Letter:

> I felt great when I was able to do _____
> for _____, whom I really care about.

You can make this a great year because you are now in touch with what really energizes you to take action. Good for you!

Step 3: Power-mations – Convert Your Letter to Affirmations

An affirmation is a statement that positively activates your conscious mind. When you effectively construct the affirmation, you can activate your subconscious mind and intuition. To do that, your affirmation needs to be positive, in the present tense and personal (the 3 Ps).

Here is an example of a well-constructed affirmation:

Your Great Year Letter

Dear _____,
_{friend's name}

Let me tell you about how terrific 20_____ was! I enjoyed
_{year}

_____. I had
identify a very pleasant highlight

a breakthrough regarding _____
identify a watershed event

_____and was surprised

at how _____,
identify an unexpected turn of events

turned out tremendously well for me. This is what happened:

_____.
describe that turn of events

The goals I set and achieved were _____
list those objectives that came to fruition

_____. Fulfilling these goals has made a difference

in my life by _____.
list the ways

The resources that helped me fulfill them were _____
list names and/or processes

_____. Finally, for the first time,

I attempted _____, successfully.
list inaugural attempts

I feel so excited about _____

identify something you anticipate greatly

_____, so proud that _____

identify a source of pride

_____, so relieved

about _____,

identify the resolution of a source of great anxiety

and finally at peace about _____.

identify something you have accepted after extended resistance

I felt deeply cared for by _____

name a supportive person, resource, or perspective

_____. I felt especially

loved when _____. I feel

identify compassionate emotional highlight

stronger and more capable regarding _____

describe an area of empowerment or growth

_____.

It was so fun to _____, and I

list positive emotional highlight

felt great when I was able to benefit _____

name of someone you helped

by doing _____.

list most beneficial thing you did for another

In conclusion, I felt most alive when _____

identify the most life affirming moment of the year

_____.

© *Tom Marcoux*   *www.TomSuperCoach.com*

I easily write Web site text that is compelling and that gets thousands of people to order my excellent products.

Positive: "easily write" and "excellent"

Present tense: "write" and "gets"

Personal: 'I'

Some people try to repeat a vague, general affirmation, such as, "I feel terrific." A number of individuals have reported that merely repeating the phrase "I feel terrific" does not modify their mood. "Affirmations don't always work," they say. Have you had this type of experience? Keep reading and I'll show you how to make real progress in your life.

Because some traditional forms of constructing and using affirmations don't seem to work, we're going to raise the process to a higher level. Remember Albert Einstein's comment, "You can never solve a problem on the level on which it was created."

The next level is to access your intuition by adding a simple question – How?

When George said to himself, "I feel terrific! How?" his mind rushed about to find answers.

- By playing my favorite music CD.

- By calling my best friend and talking about a new idea for my novel.

The point is that just mindlessly repeating an affirmation doesn't have power until you attach answers to the question, What does this take?

Another way to phrase the question is this – What does it take *for me to take action?* For example:

> *I easily write text that is compelling and that gets thousands of people to order my excellent products.*

What does this take?

1. I need to read books on how to write compelling text.

2. When ideas surface from my intuition, I drop whatever I'm doing and write them down.

3. I get access to people who already have e-newsletter subscriber lists. The lists have at least 5,000 subscribers.

4. I need to increase my credibility so that my Web site means something to the visitor.

5. I share my work with colleagues and friends to obtain compelling testimonials.

I have just given you the beginning of a process I call the *Power-mation.** A Power-mation is better than standard affirmation because it solves a difficulty that a number of people encounter with standard affirmations. Some people find that simply saying "I feel terrific" when they clearly do not feel well is like lying to oneself. The improvement is to say, "I feel terrific! How? By calling my friend; or by listening to relaxing music …"

• •

* A combination of Power and Affirmation, it could as well refer to Automation, as it encompasses the idea of automatically going to the place (or state of being) of power.

The Third Part of the Power-mation is "I Relax into ..."

Breakthroughs can be achieved through relaxation

Would you like to be a happy achiever? The happy achiever realizes that life satisfaction often includes the ability to relax and let go. A third part of the Power-mation is, "I relax into ..." The idea is to allow oneself to flow comfortably with life as it is. For example, I can try to force myself to write, or I can relax into my natural writing rhythms. I *easily write* when I write upon first waking in the morning. After an hour or so, I may feel fatigued, or writing "just doesn't feel fun anymore." Then, I switch gears to exercise or work on something else. Later in the day, I feel refreshed and I start writing again. In this way, *I relax into* writing for two or more sessions.

You cannot solve some things with action. To feel calm and peaceful, focus on "I relax into ..."

Now it's your turn. Pull out your copy of *Your Great Year Letter* and use it to help you fill in the following form.

In this chapter, you have used unusual ways to define success and set up goals for yourself.

Power-mations Boost Your Power Using Your Physiology

You unleash your hidden power when you add *compelling feeling* to your Power-mation. You do this by saying your Power-mation aloud and moving your body. For example, my client, Haro, taps his lightly closed fist on his right thigh and says *with feeling,* "I can do this! I can do this!" This process helps him shift to a state in which he is focused and energetic. You can get the same valuable results.

Power-mations for Your Great Year

Example: I easily write Web site text that is compelling and that gets people to order my excellent products.

Power-mation 1:

I _____ to _____, and I know I have
    _{verb}   _{items, people, places}

results when _____.
           _{event(s)}

What does this take?

I take action to:

I relax into:

Power-mation 2:

I _____ to _____, and I know I have
    _{verb}   _{items, people, places}

results when _____.
           _{event(s)}

What does this take?

I take action to:

I relax into:

Power-mation 3:

I _____ to _____, and I know I have
    _{verb}   _{items, people, places}

results when _____.
           _{event(s)}

What does this take?

I take action to:

I relax into:

Now, in your personal journal, write your Power-mation. Then answer this question – *What words and what physical action will I use to add compelling feeling to my Power-mation?*

~~~~~~~~~~

A crucial benefit of Build the Castle First is that it helps you gain access to your intuition.

How? The Build the Castle First Process includes asking emotionally charged questions that become an in-road to your intuition.

Another piece of accessing your intuition is the *Mission Caption.*

Step 4: A Powerful Tool – the Mission Caption

Some authors emphasize the need to write a Mission Statement. How many people have memorized their mission statement?

We live on the QuickBreakthrough Level with the help of what I call the *Mission Caption.* It can appear like a caption below a photograph.

This is my Mission Caption, "*I help people experience enthusiasm, love, and wisdom to fulfill big dreams."*

This Mission Caption, which I have memorized, helps me gain access to my intuition. Automatically, I view any opportunity from the viewpoint, "Does this opportunity assist me to help people experience enthusiasm, love, and wisdom to fulfill big dreams?"

The Mission Caption provides clarity. The value of clarity is supported by a comment from Roy O. Disney (Walt Disney's business partner and brother). Roy said, "Decision-making is easy if your values are clear." Having a Mission Caption is a valuable part of the process, *Build the Castle First.*

Memorize Your Mission Caption!

My client, Mira, wrote this Mission Caption, "I express my creativity and people feel good." She feels that this Mission Caption supports her as a business owner and a loving person.

Let the beauty of what you love be what you do.

RUMI

Write two rough drafts of your Mission Caption in your personal journal.

Now, Mike Robbins invites us to expand our life by being bold.

Be Bold

MIKE ROBBINS

Do you consider yourself bold? Some of us do, but most people I know and work with, myself included, admit that they don't often think of themselves as a bold person. Or, if we've done or said bold things in our lives, they seem to be few and far between...and they also seem to scare us half to death. Hence, we often don't find ourselves being old in life – or not nearly as much as we'd like.

Being bold, while scary and challenging for many of us, is essential if we're going to live an authentic life. Boldness is about stepping up and stepping out onto our "edge" in life – pushing the limits of what we think is possible or appropriate. It's about living, speaking, and acting in ways that are both courageous and true to who we really are.

Because we're all unique, our individual versions of boldness will look quite different. Something that might be "bold" for me, may not be so for you – or vice versa. Being bold has to do with us getting in touch with our deepest truths, passions, and desires in life and then having the courage to live and act "out loud" in a way that is congruent with this.

Here are five key reminders of what it takes to be bold in life:

1. **Be True to Yourself** – Tell and live your truth with courage, vulnerability, and commitment. We must also remain in a constant inquiry with ourselves about who we are and what's important to us.

It's okay and necessary in this process to admit when we've made a mistake, gone off course, or done something that's out of integrity for with ourselves, as well as if we feel totally lost (which we will at times). Being true to who we are is about being ruthlessly honest and forgiving with ourselves (and with others) in a way that is both fierce and compassionate.

2. **Live with Passion** – Passion comes from within us, not from the external circumstances, events, activities, or people in our lives.

Being bold is about going for it, not holding back, and giving ourselves fully to our work, our relationships, and our lives. To do this we must generate authentic passion, which is both a powerful emotion as well as a state of being as well.

3. **Step Out** – Challenge yourself to say and do things that are outside of your comfort zone and that scare you. This will force you to "step out" in your life and step in to who you really are. We often don't think we're "ready," we sometimes don't know exactly what we're supposed to do, and we almost never have a guarantee that things will work out. So what! As Ray Bradbury famously said, "Jump, and build your wings on the way down."

4. **Lean on Others** – Support, inspiration, and accountability from other people are essential along our journey of boldness and authenticity. We can't do it all by ourselves and it's imperative that we reach out to others who believe in us, will tell us the truth, and can help us when we get stuck. Create a "dream team" of powerful and supportive people around you who you can share your hopes, dreams, and ideas with. And, be willing to ask for and receive their support, contribution, and generosity.

5. **When You Fall Down, Get Back Up** – It's important to make peace with the fact that you will fall down, probably a lot, if you're really going for it and playing big in life. How we respond to falling down is what truly makes the difference in our lives. When we make a commitment to ourselves to get back up, dust ourselves off, be real about how we feel and what happened, and not let it stop us from being who we are and going for what we want – we tap into what true power, boldness, and authenticity are all about!

Mike Robbins, CSP, is a bestselling author, sought-after motivational keynote speaker, and personal growth expert who works with Fortune 500 companies, non-profits, schools, and groups and people of all kinds. He and his work have been featured on ABC News, the Oprah radio network, in *Forbes*, and many others. His books have been translated into eight different languages.

To learn more about his work, check out: www.Mike-Robbins.com

---

Mike reminds us to challenge ourselves to step outside our comfort zone so that we can experience a life of authenticity and fulfillment.

Remember that through this book, we are seeking *breakthroughs* for you. Breakthroughs energize you and help you increase your stamina so that *nothing can stop you this year.*

Principle:

Build the Castle First.

Power Question:

Where can you put *Your Great Year Letter* so you see it daily? (Examples: bathroom mirror, wall calendar, day planner, purse, wallet, near your telephone, next to your shoes, or anywhere else.)

3

Energize

The Power Up – Slim Down Program

To make this *Your Best Year Ever*, you need energy. This chapter helps you build physical stamina so you can make your dreams come true.

Where does your personal energy come from? A lot comes from appropriate food and exercise. For years, audience members listening to my speeches have asked, "Tom, do you have a diet book? Do you have a book on losing weight?"

I answer those questions below. You will get truthful, proven methods to improve your energy – and your appearance!

Part 1: Secrets for Losing Weight

(*Get lighter*)

(*As with all programs of exercise and weight control, check with your doctor or with more than one doctor.*)

Researchers note that getting to one's ideal weight boils down to four words, "Eat less. Move more."*

The Power Up – Slim Down Program

The idea is for you to feel great and look great. That leads us to our G.R.E.A.T. Process:

> G – Get clear
>
> R – Reform your exercise
>
> E – Empower your eating
>
> A – Align your food
>
> T – Transform the inner you

Get Clear

G   Write down a clear description of the exact outcomes you
R   want. To energize your efforts, it is crucial to have clear goals
E   that are related to your deeply held feelings. Many people
A   approach weight loss and health practices with the desire to be
T   physically attractive. If that is your primary goal, connect with
your feelings.

An important note – Let's take a moment to reflect on the fact that our personal optimal health and appearance may look

••••••••••••••••••••••••••••••••

* U.S. Department of Health and Human Services and National Institutes of Health emphasize, "If your health care provider tells you that you should lose weight and you want to find a weight-loss program to help you, look for one that is based on regular physical activity and an eating plan that is balanced, healthy, and easy to follow."

different from the starved fashion model look. A number of health professionals comment that a "starved lifestyle" does not foster energy and good health. The good news is that glowing skin, a toned-body and a big smile are always attractive.

Perfect *six-pack* abdominal muscles may not be a match for your lifestyle. A male model told me that before photo-shoots, he would only eat soup to get *six-pack abs*. That sounds rough. Perhaps your primary goal is being healthy and energetic.

Getting clear mentally helps you maintain your body weight. When you have a clear goal that *works for you as an individual,* you are empowered to accomplish your personal goal. One part of this process is identifying your *Red Alert Weight* and knowing what immediate action-steps you will take if you fall back to your Red Alert Weight.

Use a Red Alert Weight to Maintain Your Ideal Weight

A *Red Alert Weight* is a weight that disturbs you. For some people, it might be 140 pounds; for others, 160 or 180 pounds. This depends on your gender and body structure. (Your doctor has a chart that identifies "body mass," which you can use in your calculations.)

Using the Red Alert Weight, you avoid weighing yourself every day. Every couple of days is better, because you avoid the emotional rollercoaster of weighing yourself daily. Our weight tends to fluctuate by a few pounds anyway. When you find that you have gone over your Red Alert Weight, have the habit of going into action to get below that weight.

In the past, when I noticed that I had reached a Red Alert Weight, I took immediate action:

1. I log my food intake ("half a bowl of salad, half chicken breast").

2. I drink more water (up to 6 eight-ounce glasses) throughout the day.

3. I avoid eating after 9 p.m.

4. I often double my exercise.

I do *not* deny myself particular foods. I just eat less of them. Be careful. If you starve yourself, the body will hold calories. Instead, modify the type and amount of food you consume.

Reform Your Exercise

G   By reform, I mean *recreate* your exercise. Make it into a new
R   form. For example, I wrote the first draft of this chapter while
E   typing on my laptop computer and riding a stationary bicycle. I
A   make exercise a required part of my day. If I have had a long day
T   and I want to avoid intense exercise that could disturb my sleep, I might walk for 30 minutes inside my home.

Often, I feel great after riding my stationary bicycle, perspiring freely, and writing projects like this during the first part of my day. My daily exercise varies – I may run with a friend, ride a bicycle, do martial arts kicking or tap dance. Every night, I log in my journal that I did some form of exercise. I feel proud of myself for making exercise a priority and following through on my good intention.

A powerful benefit of exercise is that you feel more energy – that is, *you energize your life.*

An important part of reforming your exercise is to *get the pain out!* For many of us, the phrase "No pain – no gain!" translates to "Some pain – no way!" I am very strategic about my exercise. I often combine it with something I like to do. For example, I like to read, and I can read while exercising if I use a bookstand and a treadmill. I like to listen to empowering, educational audio programs. A running track is located near my home, so I listen and learn while running outside in the invigorating air!

Empower Your Eating

Eating well can empower you. It can give you the energy and stamina that enables you to squeeze life like an orange and get all the juice to enjoy.

Find ways to enjoy increasing your knowledge about nutrition. Listening to an audio program in the car or reading a book while waiting before an appointment can be helpful.

Some Key Ideas Related to Nutrition

1. Nutritionists note that nutritional supplements are crucial for optimal health. Researchers note that our current food supply contains less nutritional value than it did years ago.* Dr. Jack Groppel notes the value of

· ·

* "The 'genetic dillution effect,' in which selective breeding to increase crop yield has led to declines in protein, amino acids, and as many as six minerals in one study of commercial wheats grown in 1996 and '97 in South Carolina. Because nearly 90% of dry matter is carbohydrates, 'when breeders select for high yield, they are, in effect, selecting mostly for high carbohydrate with no assurance that dozens of other nutrients and thousands of phytochemicals

suppliers like Shaklee, Interior Design Nutritionals and Anti-Diet Vitamins/Mineral Supplements.

2. Drink water throughout the day. A number of experts recommend eight 8-ounce glasses a day. At the moment, this is controversial. Certain researchers say that you are hydrated if you see that your urine is clear.*

3. Devote time for deep breathing exercises that increase oxygen intake, which helps the body function better and metabolize nutrition more effectively.** My Affirm-Breathing Process follows this pattern.

• •

will all increase in proportion to yield.' " Donald R. Davis, "Declining Fruit and Vegetable Nutrient Composition: What Is the Evidence?," *Journal of HortScience,* February 2009, p5.

* "The average human body contains between 45 percent and 75 percent water. Every cell, tissue, and organ needs water to function properly. Water also regulates body temperature, transports nutrients and oxygen to cells. Extension consumer sciences agent. Water is the primary ingredient of all bodily fluids, including blood, saliva, gastric juices, and urine. Typical daily water output is between eight and ten cups, noted Kirkpatrick... The easiest way to monitor hydration levels is to check urine. Dark colored urine means people are not drinking enough water. Pale or colorless urine signals adequate hydration. Water intake and output should be more carefully monitored in infants, young children, older adults, athletes, pregnant and breastfeeding women, individuals who are sick, and people who undergo strenuous work or exercise." From article in *Sun Advocate* by Julene Reese.

** Increased oxygen uptake increases the metabolic rate, as more oxygen is available to the mitochondrial respiratory chain.

Affirm-Breathing Process

- Breathe in through your nose and repeat an affirmation in your mind. (Examples: "I feel peaceful" or "God relaxes me.")

- Repeat the affirmation once while holding your breath.

- Breathe out through your mouth while repeating the affirmation twice in your mind.

- Repeat the process ten times.

---

4. Add antioxidants to your diet. Antioxidants help your body avoid many of the breakdown processes of aging. Dr. Jack Groppel recommends being certain to get significants amount of Vitamins A, C, and E, plus Selenium.

Note: As with any program, consult health professionals including your doctor before you begin. Each person's current health level and requirements are unique. A number of data sources are used in this program including, *Anti-Diet Book* by Jack L. Groppel, PhD and *Get with the Program!* by Bob Greene.

Important note: Avoid overdoses of vitamin and mineral supplements, because health problems can be created including loss of hair, diarrhea, or worse. At WebMD.com, Daniel DeNoon interviewed dietitian Nancy Anderson, RD, MPH, in his article "Health-Food-Store Safari." Anderson, an expert on heart-healthy food and coordinator of the nutrition program for the Emory University Heart Center in Atlanta, commented:

> "As we age our needs change, our absorption rates for different vitamins change, and so a multivitamin that has 100% of the daily allowance of most vitamins really can help… Some people might also benefit from things like a calcium supplement, especially as you get older and have problems processing vitamin D. Calcium and vitamin D work in tandem, and so those are some supplements that benefit people. People were always told they need to get a lot of iron, and one thing we now know is that too much iron can be a bad thing, especially in terms of heart disease. Postmenopausal women, or older men don't need iron supplements. So when you are choosing a multivitamin, try to choose one with low or no iron."

Anderson also said, "Five years ago cardiologists typically recommended supplementing with [vitamins] C and E, and now they are backing off because high doses or high levels of those antioxidants have the opposite effect. They become pro-oxidative and cause coronary damage. Talk to your doctor, talk to a dietitian, and make sure you are not just buying stuff that hurts you when you are trying to do yourself some good."

Keep a journal about how you feel based on your nutritional habits. Remember, we want to energize your life. I have noticed that I feel better when I drink more water during the day. Several years ago, one of my clients noted that he felt sluggish after eating a hamburger from a fast food restaurant. Since then, he has avoided hamburgers.

A vital tip: Avoid skipping meals, because your body gets fooled into thinking it is experiencing a famine. At that point, your metabolism slows down. A fast metabolism releases fat. So consider three small meals and two appropriate snacks. Dr. Jack Groppel emphasizes that a healthy snack between lunch and dinner will help curb the tendency to overeat during dinner.

Align Your Food

When I say *align your food*, I mean align food with a healthy and uplifting part of your life. If food is too big in your life, it can trample what you really want. For example, Oprah Winfrey said that she associated comfort with food, and that she remembers the comfort provided by many foods her grandmother prepared. (Many of grandma's foods had high levels of fat.)

Similarly, years ago, I rewarded myself with the treat of an ice cream cone after jogging. I realized that rewarding myself with food was a harmful pattern. This was not positively aligning food with my personal goals. Instead, I now prefer to reward myself with a hot bath and reading in the tub.

It is helpful to be conscious of how we use food in our lives to change how we feel. We use food or drinks to raise our energy levels. For example, some of us stay up too late and eat while watching late night TV. A solution is to stay out of the television room (and away from the kitchen) late at night.

Nutritionists note that a candy bar gives a temporary lift that ends with an energy crash. I now prefer to ear carrots, raisins, tomatoes, oranges, and bananas (with a smear of peanut butter for an appropriate amount of protein) instead of packaged snack items (potato chips, etc.) I also prefer to keep half-gallons of ice cream outside my home. Anytime I truly want ice cream, I'd rather walk to the store for it. The inconvenience helps me stay fit and trim.

In a nutshell: To transform your relationship with food, I suggest developing your *Tool Kit of Rewards.* Reward yourself, increase your comforts and strive to leave food out. A number of people find that activities related to their spiritual path* provide comfort and strength.

Take the next 20 seconds to write down seven ways to reward yourself without food. This will form *Your Tool Kit of Rewards.*

Let's face this fact – If you're not having enough fun and comfort in your life outside of food, it is much too easy to fall back on food for comfort.

Keep a copy of *Your Tool Kit of Rewards* with you at all times. If music helps you feel better, keep your MP3 player in your purse, backpack, or briefcase.

My clients have written down these rewards:

1. Listening to my favorite music

2. Taking a walk in the park

3. Calling my dear friend (or sister)

4. Watching a movie

5. Knitting

••••••••••••••••••••••••••••••••••••

* For helpful ideas and methods, please see my books *Wake Up Your Spirit to Prosperity* and *Wake Up Your Spirit to Prosperity for Couples.*

6. Luxuriating in a hot bath

7. Devoting time to my hobby

8. Tap dancing

9. Doing many other activities

A tip: My closest friends are accustomed to my habit of getting a take-out box in a restaurant at the beginning of the meal. This habit helps me eat only half of the portion placed before me.

Another tip: I do not deny myself the taste of foods I enjoy. Instead, I change the quantities. For example, my sweetheart and I share a dessert in a restaurant.

Transform the Inner You

What we look to transform is our relationship with our inner child. Psychologists call the inner child our source of energy. Researchers have noted that when we constantly deny ourselves joy, our inner child rebels and acts out.* Acting out may include a food binge. To avoid an inner child rebellion, I find it useful to write (in my journal) a dialogue between my inner parent and inner child. Since I am quite productive, my inner parent exerts a lot of control. To create balance, I devote quiet time to writing in my journal. This allows me to reflect on what would bring joy to my playful side.

G
R
E
A
T

• •

* There are a number of resources that address working with the inner child. *Inner Bonding: Becoming a Loving Parent to Your Inner Child*, Dr. Margaret Paul is a well-received book based on her counseling work.

Remember that the inner child is the part of you that may feel vulnerable or small and that wants to have fun. The inner child is important because it provides the energy you need to improve your life.

What happens when you become skillful in nurturing your inner child? You transform the inner you from a scared and begging inner child to a safe and joyful inner child. This form of inner child (or inner you) becomes generous and gives you energy to fulfill your big dreams.

In a nutshell: To transform your relationship with the inner you, devote time to discovering what brings you joy (so that you have other sources besides food). Then, take action and increase your daily quota of joyful moments. Some of my clients enjoy their exercise in these ways:

1. Strolling to the park and riding on swings

2. Walking around Toys"R"Us

3. Walking at an amusement park with nephews and nieces

In your personal journal, list seven things that answer the question – *What brings me joy?*

The Power Up – Slim Down Program

Part 2: Exercise

Seven keys to consistent exercise

For years, my father, Al Marcoux, has exercised every day. He uses a calendar to note his activities, including in-line skating, pushing my mother in her wheelchair for a mile or more, doing sit-ups, doing aerobic exercise on a Healthrider, running for 30 minutes to 2 hours, performing knee-strengthening exercises and walking 2 miles with a friend. He says that he was never an athlete, and he began running at 47. He started to complete 26-mile marathons at age 54 (and has finished 12 marathons so far).

His example shows us that it's never too late to begin any worthwhile activity, including physical exercise.

How to feel great

Feeling happy usually occurs when we feel good physically. As we become older, exercise is necessary to stay healthy and feel young. Researchers have proven that exercise can reverse the undesirable effects often associated with aging.* Bad moods

· ·

* "Exercise improves your mood… Physical activity stimulates various brain chemicals that may leave you feeling happier and more relaxed than you were before you worked out… Exercise combats chronic diseases. Worried about heart disease? Hoping to prevent osteoporosis? Physical activity might be the ticket. Regular physical activity can help you prevent – or manage – high blood pressure. Your cholesterol will benefit, too. Regular physical activity boosts high-density lipoprotein (HDL), or 'good,' cholesterol while decreasing triglycerides. This one-two punch keeps your blood flowing smoothly by lowering the buildup of plaques in your arteries. And there's more. Regular physical activity can help you prevent type 2 diabetes, osteoporosis and certain types of cancer… Exercise helps you manage your weight… Physical activity delivers oxygen and nutrients to your tissues. In fact, regular physical activity helps your entire cardiovascular system – the circulation of blood through your heart and blood vessels – work more efficiently. Big deal? You bet! When your heart and lungs work more efficiently, you'll have more energy to do the things you enjoy… Exercise promotes better sleep." From "Exercise: 7 benefits of regular physical activity" by Mayo Clinic staff.

have been shown to result from tired bodies and minds. Just 10 or 15 minutes of aerobic exercise will change bad moods to happier ones. *Exercise helps us feel great!*

Earlier in this chapter, we discussed writing in a personal journal and listing seven things that answer the question – *What brings you joy?*

Some of my clients find that small activities bring joyful moments:

1. Knitting

2. Painting a picture

3. Going on a photo-safari (walking with a friend or loved one in various parks or other places and taking digital photos)

Many of us find that feeling great involves new sights, sounds, and places. A brief day-trip to a nearby city can be refreshing.

How can you start and continue an exercise program?

Many people do *not* have exercise on their schedule because they have *not* devoted time to think through the keys that help maintain an exercise program. In this chapter, we explore a process that really works.

Here are seven keys to help make your exercise an I-want-to-do part of your busy life. The following keys are based on the *Optimal Exercise Chart* (found on page 51), which is part of my seminar for corporations entitled *Be Happy and Fit While You're Busy.*

Focus on maintaining a regular exercise program. Our process is R.E.G.U.L.A.R.

R – Reason out visible results

E – Energize variety

G – Go for a short time

U – Unleash enjoyment

L – Lean on an easy system

A – Arrange convenience

R – Regulate feelings

Reason Out Visible Results

When I emphasize *reason out*, I mean that we need to set reasonable projections for visible results. Caroline has been an on-and-off exercise person for years – mostly off. She felt that the visible results of weight loss were coming too slowly for the efforts she was putting in.

A useful example for us is the reasonable schedule used by Zig Ziglar, bestselling author and national speaker. His extended schedule included something like reducing 3 pounds per month over a period of 10 months. Researchers note that lean muscle tissue weighs more than fatty tissue, so weight is not a prime indicator of fitness.* However, Zig Ziglar's experience

R
E
G
U
L
A
R

••••••••••••••••••••••••••••••••

* "Get started with the simple assessment guidelines below – [from] the President's Challenge, an activity program designed by the President's Council on Physical Fitness and Sports ... [1] Check your aerobic fitness: Brisk walk ... [2] Measure muscular fitness: Push-ups ... [3] Assess your

demonstrates the principle of setting up *reasonable* projections for visible results.

Energize Variety

R
E
G
U
L
A
R

Angela became bored with various forms of exercise, such as bicycling, running, and walking. She had chosen one activity at a time with a must-do approach and a rigid schedule. On the other hand, Rebecca varies her exercises from day to day, and this makes them more interesting to her. From Monday to Thursday, she selects one of these: (a) follow an exercise video; (b) walk; (c) run; (d) ride a stationary bicycle. On Fridays, she enjoys ballroom dancing.

• •

flexibility: Sit-and-reach test ... [4]Estimate your body composition: Waist circumference and body mass index." From "How fit are you? See how you measure up" by the Mayo Clinic staff.

Optimal Exercise Chart™		
Plan	*Action*	*Result*
Reason out visible results	example: lose 3 lbs. per month	example: lost 2 lbs. per month for 4 months
Energize variety		
Go for a short time		
Unleash enjoyment		
Lean on an easy system		
Arrange convenience		
Regulate feelings		

Go for a Short Time

Trisha finds that she devotes 40 minutes to driving to and from the fitness center, 20 minutes to changing clothes and an hour to working out. No wonder she procrastinates! As an alternative, you can include short time-period activities in your schedule: a 20-minute walk, a 20-minute session using an exercise video, a 30-minute jog or 10 minutes using hand-weights. Many people exercise during part of their lunch hour. Another time-saver is combining exercise with another activity. You can walk with a friend. When riding a stationary bicycle, you can enjoy watching TV or listening to an educational audio program.

Unleash Enjoyment

R
E
G
U
L
A
R
Remember the last time you procrastinated doing a task? Did you imagine how painful or inconvenient the task was going to be? Then, did you find that you didn't feel like doing it at all? The solution is to make exercise an *enjoyable* part of your daily life. You can enjoy exercise by combining something soothing with your exercise: (a) music (b) talking with a friend; (c) watching TV; or (d) reading (when using a stationary bicycle or treadmill).

Lean on an Easy System

R
E
G
U
L
A
R
Use an easy system. One principle is, *When you want to improve it, measure it.* It is vital to use an easy system so you can see your consistent efforts.

Marcus does not do this. He writes a note about exercise in his day planner, but at a glance, he has no idea how often he exercises in a given week. A better example is my father, Al. He uses a calendar that he keeps near the bathroom sink. Each day, he notes any physical activity he has accomplished, such as: RN – run; WK – substantial walk; SU – sit-ups; or other exercise abbreviations. He counts each day a plus when any activity is recorded and always knows how his exercise program is progressing.

Clarity helps you *feel* your progress, and this is motivating. You can use a *Self-Leadership Chart* that looks like this:

Self-Leadership Chart™	Mon	Tues	Wed	Thu	Fri	Sat	Sun
Check this chart	√	√	√	√	√	√	√
10 minutes with hand weights		√	√		√		
Walk with a friend	√		√	√			
20-minute walk at lunchtime	√	√	√				
20 minutes with an exercise video					√	√	

Be sure to view your chart daily. This keeps the major tasks in mind so that you won't let two days go by without doing something positive. Also, give yourself a reward for each time you exercise. A reward could be simply taking time to watch a pre-recorded television show. A number of my clients find it helpful to post the chart in a place where they must see it, such as on the bathroom mirror.

Arrange Convenience

Charley is often heard to say, "This week, I really need to get to the gym." Of course, he doesn't always make it. It is the inconvenience of going to and from the gym and waiting for the

R
E
G
U
L
A
R

equipment to be free that hold him back. On the other hand, my father simply steps outside for his run, and I ride my stationary bicycle while typing on my laptop.

Regulate Feelings

R
E
G
U
L
A
R

By saying *regulate feelings*, we focus on creating situations in which you feel good.

My father knows how good he feels after a run. On the other hand, Jim felt discouraged when he noticed that the inches were not melting away from his stomach area after two weeks of hard exercise, but he *benefited in other ways*. Researchers emphasize that people who exercise feel better because exercise releases endorphins.* Endorphins are natural pain-relieving and stress-reducing substances in our blood stream. Knowing this helps us understand the value of targeting the feelings we want to gain. Just using hand weights for a few days will help our arms feel stronger. Thus, good feelings are gained from strength training.

Remember that *appropriate food and exercise* truly improve your personal energy.

Sleep is important, too. In fact, recent studies have revealed that lack of sleep is connected to weight-gain. I invite you to learn more about healthy sleep habits.

· ·

* "Your body will … release endorphins, natural painkillers that promote an increased sense of well-being." From "Aerobic Exercise: Top 10 reasons to get physical," by Mayo Clinic staff.

*Four of five people are more in
need of rest than exercise.*

DR. LOGAN CLENDENING

Principle:

Transform your relationship with food, exercise, and get in touch with the inner you.

Power Questions:

What simple details related to appropriate food and exercise would help you take better care of yourself? What can you do today to start your process of self-nurturing?

4

Surround Yourself with the Compelling

Imagine that you can do what you previously thought impossible. How about making your impossible dreams come true?

When you *surround yourself with the compelling*, you *automatically go into action*. In this chapter, you will learn to use the *TriggerSet Method*™, which helps you create the momentum that originates success and fulfillment.

The *Random House Dictionary* defines *to compel* as "to force or drive, especially to a course of action ... to overpower ... to have a powerful and irresistible effect, influence." We want to overpower inertia, low moods, and procrastination. We want to consistently go into action to create the best for our life.

Anthony Robbins said, "It's not that life is boring, it's *you* that's boring ... You have impotent goals."* With impotent

....

* Goals can be impotent because (1) they do not have one's deepest desire as the first cause, or (2) the goal is actually someone else's goal – for example, saxophonist Kenny G's mother wanted him to get a college degree in

goals, many people live a life of disappointment.

But you can have a better life than that! Join the people who create a fulfilling life. These achievers have found ways to make taking action a *compelling* part of life. They feel *a pull* to reach for more and better – and to learn how to make that happen.

rendered by Chris Sehenuk

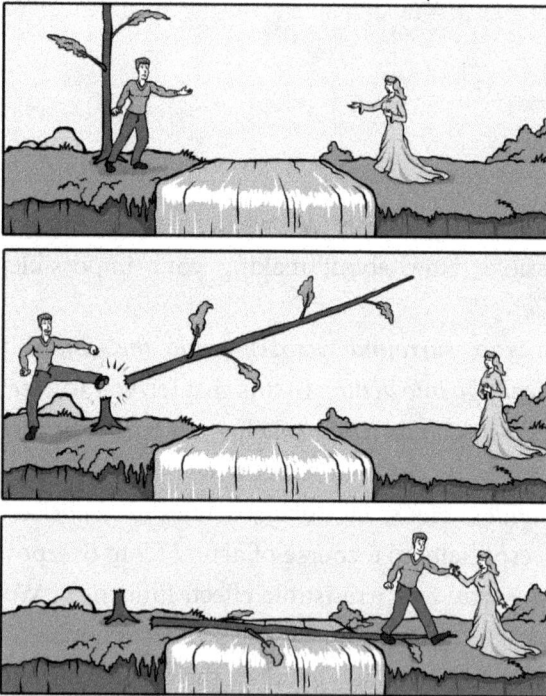

With the right incentive, Nothing Can Stop You!

something "practical." Research demonstrates that people lose resolve or interest in stretching themselves to pursue goals that do not arise from their personal core.

Along these lines, I invite you to *surround yourself with the compelling*. In a few moments, I'll share with you the *12 elements of the compelling*. But first, you'll learn a process that my clients have found essential in order to do something that made a huge difference in their lives. This process is the *TriggerSet Method*™. Using this method, my clients have dropped extra weight, written books and completed other life-changing activities.

What do you want to do? What do you need to do to break out of any rut you may find yourself in?

From birth, we are conditioned to respond to triggers. Mom smiles and we're happy. Dad frowns and we're concerned.

Now is your chance to take control of your own life.

TriggerSet Method™

This is a breakthrough process, because we use physiology and we don't rely on willpower. It goes as fast as:

Eyes see ▥➡ Feeling in the body ▥➡ Action!

The idea is that triggers, events that prompt a predictable, but undesired, response in us, can be reprogrammed. To do so, before exposing ourselves to triggering events, we define an alternate beneficial *trigger response sequence*. For example, if a student finds that seeing the Discussion Topics page of an online class causes feelings such as, "I feel tired, it's already been a long day," the student does better to have another response pre-planned. She can have energizing music ready in her iPod so that she can listen to this music to "power up" so that she efficiently posts comments onto the Discussion Topics page.

The TriggerSet Method™ Worksheet

1. Copy, fold, & tape, forming a hollow prism, as shown.
2. Complete blanks on left immediately.
3. Log results over time on right.

- - - - - - - - - - - - - - -

Fold here

www.TomSuperCoach.com   © Tom Marcoux

- - - - - - - - - - - - - - -

Fold here

OUTCOME desired:

Log of Results:
date – specific action

ACTION you must take:

TRIGGER which initiates action:

TRIGGERSET METHOD™

- - - - - - - - - - - - - - -

Tape here

Fold here

- - - - - - - - - - - - - -

Cut here

As another example, I have used the trigger of a portable sign that reads, "Only water 9 p.m. – 6 a.m." This is a positive trigger. It tells me exactly what the healthy thing is to do. It does not dwell on "food" or "hunger pains."

> *When you are thinking clearly,*
> *set triggers so you will act automatically.*

This entire section, *Surround Yourself with the Compelling*, is about being strategic with the triggers that you set.

Log Your Results

An important element of the TriggerSet Method™ is keeping a log of results.

TriggerSet Method™ for Sales

My client, Cherie, puts a small sign on her computer monitor, "Call 4 Prospects before 11 a.m." She also writes a personal reward, "Calling for 5 days equals a new music album."

The power of the TriggerSet Method™ is clarity and simplicity.

~~~~~~~~~~~~~~~~~~~

At this point, I will share the specifics of *Surround Yourself with the Compelling.*

The compelling includes 12 elements:

1. Your Milestones Binder

2. The inspiring work of the best in your industry

3. Your birthday celebration poster ("the doing now")

4. Books and audio programs that energize you

5. Memorized phrases

6. Project binder with a beckoning cover

7. Your easy, simple process to Keep Score and Achieve More.

8. Your process to Make It a Game You Can Win

9. Daily Journal of Victories and Blessings

10. Power of Alliances

11. Wall of Victory (or poster or corkboard)

12. Specific goal to brighten a loved one's life

12 Elements of the Compelling

1. Your Milestones Binder

Dr. Wayne Dyer said, "Some people live the same year ten times." They get stuck in a comfort zone. But a better life is available to you.

For example, my clients use a *Milestones Binder* to experience a *new year* every year. They use the Milestones Binder to celebrate what they do that is new and different in each year. Their entries include achievements such as:

- Wrote my first press release and published an article in the newspaper for the first time
- Completed a draft of my novel for the first time
- Gave a talk at a Toastmasters meeting for the first time
- Sent a book proposal to an agent for the first time
- Tried tap dancing for the first time

Your benefits from using the Milestones Binder are two-fold.

First, you give yourself acknowledgement for your dedicated efforts.

> *We must celebrate our own small victories. We cannot wait for anyone to praise us – or even to care about our personal striving for a better life. You care, so you take notice – with your Milestones Binder.*

You can give yourself a reward for each entry in your Milestones Binder.

Second, you gain incentive to stretch, grow, and try new activities. I find that I often anticipate writing my new accomplishment in the Milestones Binder – logging my efforts and giving myself credit. Then, I feel good *again* when I read the accomplishment to my romantic partner. I call that process the *Moment of Appreciation*. When she listens, I pause and say the accomplishment aloud, which helps me experience the good feelings of my personal stretching and growing.

2. The Inspiring Work of the Best in Your Industry

Who inspires you? What work gets you to say, "If I could only write (paint, make films or do something else) the way that person does!"

If you are an aspiring writer, keep copies of your favorite books near you. Look at the book covers. Glance at your favorite passages. *Know in your heart that you can accomplish great things.* Let your heroes in your industry light your path forward. For example, my client, Jack, wants to write a novel. He has a copy of Stephen King's novel *The Gunslinger*, which includes the opening line:

> *The man in black fled across the desert,*
> *and the gunslinger followed.*

Jack loves this line and it inspires him to continue his own novel writing.

You gain inspiration and energy by keeping your heroes' work at hand.

3. Your Birthday Celebration Poster

("The doing now")

Ever have a birthday and look around, saying to yourself, "This is nowhere close to how I expected my life to be at this age." It's happened to me. The good news is that the birthday celebration poster has saved me from energy-draining thoughts for many years! During the week prior to my 30th birthday, I was not happy about my life. I was nowhere near where I wanted to be. To rebel against depressive thoughts, I decided to take action and create a ritual *to celebrate what I was doing.* Now, each year in the days prior to my birthday, I write up what I am currently doing and looking forward to in the coming 12 months. Then I gather my closest friends and we celebrate what I am currently doing (with the help of my team members). I place the 8 ½ x 11-inch "poster" on a stand and launch it the way one launches a ship. I use a tube with confetti instead of a bottle of champagne. The point is that I *choose* my thoughts. I *choose to be grateful* for the blessings that are in my life now. I have learned that the joy is in the doing, and I learned to keep up my morale with a birthday celebration poster.

4. Books & Audio Programs that Energize You

Many people who accomplish extraordinary feats in life have family members and friends with no such vision. How can you devote time with *your* people – those who have similar goals and who have gone through similar trials to achieve what they want? Through books and audio programs, you are acquainted with stories of people who have done or are doing what you want to do. This is like getting together with mentors. (It is also good to find mentors who you can meet in person.)

Hearing the stories of *doers* can help you counteract the counterproductive criticism of well-intentioned family members who may try to dissuade you from taking a calculated risk. These family members may want to help you avoid the pain of disappointment. But by not taking the calculated risk, one will still experience disappointment – often the *worst* kind of disappointment, "If only I had tried, it might have worked out well. But I'll never know. And I'll die here in this rut."

Over the years, my father has said, "I don't know anything about that." *But I wanted to know about many things.* So I went outside my father's circle and learned how to produce, write, and direct feature films. I learned how to work with attorneys to draw up fair and appropriate contracts. I learned how to form and lead companies.

Another example of moving beyond the small-scope thinking of loved ones is found in the experience of multimillionaire and author, Roger Dawson. As a young person in England, Roger talked about moving to America. His friends and family (31 people) advised him to avoid going to America. Later, Roger said, "I should have asked people who had already moved to America … They would have said, 'It's great here [and there is] so much opportunity." Roger Dawson found fortune and fulfillment after he took action and moved to America.

> *Often the difference between a successful [person] and a failure is not one's better abilities or ideas, but the courage that one has to bet on his ideas, to take a calculated risk – and to act.*
>
> MAXWELL MALTZ

The calculated risk is the key. For example, if you are considering self-publishing a book, you can test the title by releasing a preliminary version as an e-book. Test the waters. That's using the power of a calculated risk.

Empowering books and audio programs offer the gift of inspiration and companionship. They enable you to make the best of your life.

5. Memorized Phrases

How can you instantly change the direction of your thoughts? With memorized phrases. When you have empowering ideas at instant recall, you can change the flow of your thinking. Thoughts inspire feelings. If you want to feel better, think better.

For years I have emphasized what I call *switch-phrases.* Imagine that your thoughts are on a train track. With an empowering switch-phrase, you can change the direction of your thoughts.

> *One can never consent to creep when one feels the impulse to soar.*
>
> HELEN KELLER

A quote can empower you. Having read Helen Keller's quote, you can ask these questions, "Am I creeping? What would soaring feel like to me? What do I need to do next to prepare to soar?"

And as I mentioned earlier, questions are the road to your intuition.

The answer is in the question. Ask better questions. What am I learning here? How can we make this better?

TOM MARCOUX

More quotes:

The superior [person] thinks always of virtue; the common man thinks of comfort.

CONFUCIUS

Let no one come to you without leaving better.

MOTHER TERESA

If you want others to be happy, practice compassion. If you want to be happy, practice compassion.

THE DALAI LAMA

Our fears must never hold us back from pursuing our hopes.

PRESIDENT JOHN F. KENNEDY

I will not die an unlived life. I will not live in fear of falling or catching fire. I choose to inhabit my days, to allow my living to open me, to make me less afraid, more accessible; to loosen my heart until it becomes a wing, a torch, a promise. I choose to risk my significance, to live so that which came to me as seed

*goes to the next as blossom, and that which came to
me as blossom, goes on as fruit.*

DAWNA MARKOVA

You can use a quote to transform your thinking and, eventually, your beliefs. Some people hold back from becoming successful because they have bought into their parents' biases that successful people are ruthless.

You can choose your personal definition of what a truly successful person does. Many of us find that "a ruthless but materially successful person" is *not* truly a success in our eyes.

Similarly, Helen, one of my clients, uses these quotes in her mind when her mother goes on a tirade "against rich people":

*Success makes [people], for the most
part, humble, tolerant, and kind. Failure
makes people bitter and cruel.*

SOMERSET MAUGHAM

*I don't know what your destiny will be, but one thing
I know: the only ones among you who will be really
happy are those who will have sought and found how
to serve.*

ALBERT SCHWEITZER

The idea is that there *are* people who are successful and kind. For example, author Richard Carlson was a kind, successful person that I knew before he passed away (when he was only 45).

Richard Carlson, author of the bestselling series *Don't Sweat the Small Stuff*, was kind to me. When we were both guests on a radio show, he took me aside and gave me some personal coaching. Now, that fits in with how I define success. Richard told me that *Don't Sweat the Small Stuff* was his tenth book. He loved to write (and I do, too), and he kept going through nine books previous to his extremely successful *Don't Sweat* series. The knowledge of this kind of success helps people.

Through empowering quotes, you change your perception of what is possible. Yes, you can be successful and kind – and a spiritual person!

Choose your quotes and memorize them. *You can empower yourself in seconds with a quote that moves your heart.*

Would you like instant inspiration when you need it? Choose quotes of people you admire. For example, you can type a person's name into the search function of BrainyQuotes.com and often see his or her famous quotes. My clients have looked up Gandhi, Mother Teresa, Walt Disney, Martin Luther King, Jr., Steve Jobs, and others.

6. Project Binder with a Beckoning Cover

Do you have a project that has been at the back of your mind? Have you wondered what you life would be like if you could just complete that novel or screenplay or some other project? Here's the solution – set up a project binder. Place your project binder on your nightstand so you can see it upon awakening in the morning. The project binder can inspire you to write for 15 minutes or more in the morning.

That's how this book was finished. Every morning, I saw the beckoning project binder, and I wrote first thing in the morning. I printed out the pages and placed them in the binder. Thus, every day I had a surge of good feelings as I saw and felt progress (pages)! The dream was coming true – step-by-step and page-by-page.

Using a project binder with a beckoning cover is another example of using the *TriggerSet Method*™. By working with the binder, we *set a trigger.* Every time we see our binder, we are likely to go into action. Using the project binder is *setting a trigger on purpose.*

7. Keep Score & Achieve More

Professional writers keep track of how many words or pages they write each day. Bestselling author John Grisham said, "If you don't write one thousand words a day, then you are not serious about writing." Stephen King notes that he aims for 2,000 words a day.

These top authors are doing a process I call *Keep Score and Achieve More.* Many authors accomplish their writing goal and then go on to enjoy the rest of day – guilt-free!

The point is that *making progress is fun.* Keeping the daily word-count helps authors feel good and energized as they successfully make progress on a daily basis.

Keeping a log of steps accomplished can help in many situations:

- Business owner/salesperson: log of phone numbers dialed, voicemails left on answering machines and prospective customers reached voice-to-voice

- Married person: log of compliments or praise given to the spouse in one week

- Continuing education student: log of textbook pages read; log of hours devoted to completing a term paper

You gain the benefit of momentum and good feelings when you set up a process to *Keep Score and Achieve More.*

8. Make It a Game You Can Win

When you make a game you can win, you can feel good every day. For example, my process of logging my daily word-count helps me make writing into a game I can win.

Susan, one of my clients, was auditioning for feature films and commercials. I guided her to keep a journal of (1) *what works* and (2) *areas to improve.* When she writes an entry in her journal, she immediately congratulates herself for what she has done well (*what works*). Then she makes a note of something she may have left out (*area to improve*). The idea is to keep up morale and learn something from each activity. Regardless of how the audition has gone, Susan *wins.* Then, she closes her journal and is free to enjoy her next activity. You, too, can enjoy these good feelings.

I have worked with a number of clients who, before working with me, had lives in which they could not win. But that's *not* for you. You need to *surround yourself with the compelling* – positive items that charge you up emotionally to take action. So, be sure to use techniques that make taking action for your dreams into a game you can win – on a daily basis!

9. Daily Journal of Victories & Blessings

Ever lie down at bedtime and feel disappointed about how little you accomplished in a particular day? When I was in college, there were nights when I went to bed and felt terrible. I felt that I was losing, that I hadn't got enough done.

To counteract that feeling, I have written every night for years in my *Daily Journal of Victories and Blessings.* Now, I go to sleep feeling grateful and blessed. I give myself acknowledgements for my daily efforts.

Often, I exercise simply because I look forward to noting that victory in my Daily Journal of Victories and Blessings. This process works so well that I tend to exercise 360 days a year.

In my journal, I often write down that I have talked with friends and family members. Those moments on the phone are blessings in my life.

Too many journals & binders for you?

Perhaps you feel that keeping Your Milestone Binder, Project binders, and Daily Journal of Victories and Blessings is too complicated. Here's the good news: this list of 12 Elements of the Compelling is really a menu. Choose any one method, use it consistently – and you win! Take action and keep going. And truly, *nothing can stop you this year!*

10. Power of Alliances

When you really want to leap forward, create alliances. Jack Canfield and Mark Victor Hansen's success soared to the stratosphere when they joined forces and created *Chicken Soup for the Soul*. Mark Victor Hansen says, "The power of 1 + 1 equals eleven."

A mastermind group is valuable. Top Internet marketer and bestselling author Joe Vitale said, "A mastermind group can help you reach any goal … A mastermind is a group, usually about six in number, and usually in non-competing businesses. They meet to help each other achieve their goals … On one level it's an obvious support group. Each person brings their own skill set, background business experience to the table, and everyone learns from another perspective. But from a Jungian perspective, you also create and tap into a larger mind, a type of third mind that is formed by a meeting of supportive people."

Joe Vitale continued, "The mastermind is run by whoever is the designated driver, so to speak. Basically, each person gets the chance to state their goals, their needs, and so forth … Our group meets every Thursday, in person, at a restaurant. But I've been in two that were done entirely over the phone. And these days you could do them over the Internet with a webcam."

An interviewer said, "Being part of a mastermind group sounds like a shortcut to greater success. What if I can't find one?"

"You can start your own mastermind group," I replied.

When I started my own Breakthrough Mastermind Group, I used this form:

Breakthrough Mastermind Group Worksheet

Conference call on first & third Mondays each month, 9:00 – 9:30 p.m.

- 2 minutes for each person to present to the group their top goal and its corresponding obstacle.
- 5 minutes for person to receive feedback from group.
- 1 minute per person to state another goal to accomplish by the next session
- Any person can initiate a call after the meeting to another group member for follow-up.

Date:

Top Goal:

Obstacle:

Next Goal to Accomplish before Next Session:

Feedback:

Details that need follow-up with any due dates:

© *Tom Marcoux   www.TomSuperCoach.com*

Delegate What You Hate
and Overcome Procrastination

Researchers note that people often procrastinate due to the anticipation of pain.* The following are powerful ideas:

- Delegate what you hate.
- If you delegate to yourself plus a friend, you have still delegated.

An interviewer asked, "What does that mean: 'delegate to music'?" I explained that if music puts you in a better mood or an energized mood, then you have "delegated" to your stronger self.

The idea of delegating to yourself plus a friend is an instance of the *Power of Alliances*. Some of my clients ask their romantic partner to help them get started on an onerous task for 15 minutes. Once the momentum is going, the partner can go on to some other activity.

Another tip: In my book, *Wake Up Your Spirit to Prosperity*, I describe the *Morning 8*. For 8 minutes in the morning, a number of my clients do an onerous task:

· ·

*Dr. Kevin P. Austin, director of the Student Counseling Services at California Institute of Technology notes, "People procrastinate because they experience emotions they don't want to feel when they attempt to do things. Those emotions can be of helplessness, powerlessness, being overwhelmed, being controlled, sad, or resentful. The reasons a person has these feelings are not addressed by procrastinating, but the feelings themselves are avoided for awhile."

taxes paperwork or tedious clearing of clutter. But they are fresh and ready every morning to take action.

When you can overcome procrastination, truly *nothing can stop you!*

11. Wall of Victory

Mark Victor Hansen (coauthor of books in the *Chicken Soup for the Soul* series and creator of numerous products) has a Wall of Victory. He has photos that document hundreds of successful details of his life, including photos of himself with various notable people. These images lift his spirits.

Similarly, you can have a Wall of Victory, or at least a poster or corkboard of victory. Kim, one of my clients, has a Corkboard of Victory. She put a corkboard on the outside of her bathroom door. Currently, she has 3x5-inch cards showing parts of her screenplay in progress. She has also posted images of her favorite films, along with an image (crafted with Adobe Photoshop software) of herself sitting next to Oprah Winfrey. She envisions becoming a major inspirational writer who is invited to be a guest on Oprah's TV show.

As part of her Corkboard of Victory, Kim has an image of herself receiving her diploma while shaking hands with the dean of the college she attended. She feels that she was able to complete college, so she can do just about anything.

You can energize yourself when you use a Wall of Victory.

12. Specific Goal to Brighten a Loved One's Life

Many of us just will *not* stretch to make our own life better. We just don't seem to be wired that way. But give a mother the chance to enhance her daughter's life, and she will move heaven and earth.

Earlier in this book, I asked: "Are you a *for-the-team* person?" Power flows when you set goals that enrich your life and your family's life. Also, some people like Oprah Winfrey set goals of giving to people who are suffering. If you have a cause (such as helping formerly battered women), you can add that to your goals.

Anthony Robbins decided that he needed to give from his financial abundance. His goal was to feed all the needy people in a particular area on Thanksgiving Day. To accomplish his goal, he needed to increase his financial abundance to the level of $4 million per year. Robbins felt the drive to take truly effective action to increase the profits of his business endeavors.

Remember, your great year (in which nothing can stop you) begins when you surround yourself with *The Compelling*.

Principle:

Surround Yourself with the Compelling.

Power Questions:

Which of the 12 Elements of the Compelling grabbed your attention? What can you do today to make that an empowering part of your life?

(For example, some of my clients use a Daily Journal of Victories and Blessings.)

5

Turn Around Your Moods

Imagine people you've met who consistently take action. Have you noticed that they have a real advantage?

These people learn how to ride out and shorten the duration of a low mood.* The solution for many of my clients is to develop a pre-planned *Low Mood First Aid Kit.*

My clients have noted these parts of their personal Low Mood First Aid Kit:

- Inspirational book

- iPod (or CD player with favorite music CD)

- Photo of his or her children

- Photo of himself or herself with romantic partner in a joyful mood in a relaxing place

- Reminders to take a walk outside, soak in a hot bath, or call loving friends

It is crucial to have certain activities that you can do on your own to elevate your mood.

Low Mood First Aid Kit Method 1

Let a Negative Thought Float Away

My client, Rana, has a recurring thought that can drain her energy in seconds: "My mother doesn't respect me or my choices. She thinks I'm an idiot." After working with me, Rana has developed a process in which she just allows that thought to flow away. She treats her thoughts like leaves floating down a stream of water. In fact, she looks for another thought immediately – something uplifting, like: "I love the comments of my students. They tell me how I helped them improve their artwork and that I have given them hope to pursue their artistic careers." I call this process the *Floating Leaves Method.*

This process of letting a negative thought float away and then choosing to focus on a positive, uplifting thought can help you live more moments in an empowered way. You'll feel better more of the time!*

Low Mood First Aid Kit Method 2

Use the Process of Write Down – Rip Up to Handle Anger

Anger can drain us of vital energy that we need to pursue our

••••••••••••••••••••••••••••••

* If you or someone you know has persistent, severe low moods, medical help may be needed. For many people, a combination of medicine and talk-therapy has proved effective for working with clinical depression.

big dreams. Years ago, when I worked in a particular corporation, a manager said something to me that was so rude, offensive, and inappropriate that my internal reaction was intense anger. Fortunately, I had heard about writing down my thoughts to get them out of my system. I added an important twist – I ripped up the page and put it in my pocket. If that manager had found my comments, I would have been shown the door!

By ripping up the page, I also ensured that I did not re-read my comments. I got them out of my system, and the rest of my day was not permanently marred by one person's momentary crass behavior.*

You now have a method to empower yourself when someone attempts to cut you down. Make the choice to use the *Write Down – Rip Up Process*, and you will strengthen yourself.

Low Mood First Aid Kit Method 3

Use a Pattern-Interrupt to Shift Out of Your Low Mood

Often, words are not enough. We need to put our body into action, which will create a ripple effect into our thoughts and feelings.

As I mentioned earlier, Haro uses a lightly closed fist tapped twice on his right thigh to *snap out* of a negative thought patterns. When he feels tired at work, he taps his closed fist and tells himself: "I can do this. I can do this."

••••••••••••••••••••••••••••••••••

* Our team has received numerous responses from people who express how they have benefited from my audio CD program: *How to Heal When Life's Too Much*. I invite you to consider this audio CD as an additional support for yourself. Available at www.TomSuperCoach.com.

The process of using his body combined with empowering words functions as a *Pattern-Interrupt* for his previous behaviors. You can choose how to interrupt self-defeating behaviors.

Identify a self-defeating behavior pattern. Write it in your journal.

Write down 2 ways to use your body and an empowering idea. (Use a *Pattern-Interrupt Process* to elevate your mood.)

Remember, low moods come and go, but we have choices for how we ride them out. We can take action to help shorten the duration of a low mood.

Principle:

Prepare a *Low Mood First Aid Kit* so that you're able to ride out a low mood and help shorten its duration.

Power Questions:

Which of the three *Low Mood First Aid Kit Methods* touched your feelings in a positive way? Which of these methods do you want to implement? List a couple of things you can do today.

6

How Billionaires & Millionaires Use B.E.S.T. Principles

H ere are
the B.E.S.T. principles, once again:

B – Build the Castle First

E – Energize

S – Surround Yourself with the Compelling

T – Turn Around Your Moods

Bill Gates

One of the founders of Microsoft, he is among the most influential technologists of the digital era.

Bill Gates used the principle of *Surround Yourself with the Compelling*. In particular he used the *Power of Alliances*. It is reported that his mother had a contact at IBM that informed her that IBM needed an operating system. Bill went to his father for a $50,000 loan so that he could buy an operating system which he then renamed as MS-DOS and licensed to IBM. With his childhood friend Paul Allen, Bill Gates formed Microsoft. Their powerful alliance showed promise in their teenage years. Bill and Paul ran a small company called Traf-O-Data and sold a computer to the city of Seattle that could count city traffic. Certainly, Bill Gates has demonstrated a lot of ability with business decisions *and* he has worked with effective associates.

Oprah Winfrey

She is one of the most powerful women in America by virtue of her immensely popular daytime talk show and magazine.

Oprah Winfrey uses the principle of Surround Yourself with the Compelling. Specifically, Oprah focuses on a *Specific Goal to Brighten a Loved One's Life.* She has chosen needy children in Africa. In 2003, she gave 50,000 gifts to needy African children. Oprah said, "There's so much sadness in the world and I wanted to be able to do something ... I wanted to be able to bring a joy to children who would not have had a day of joy. Because I remembered in my life there were times when people did that for me, so I wanted to be able to extend myself and kindness." Oprah concluded, "I feel that I have a calling. I feel that part of that calling certainly has been to be on television, and to use television in a way that can make a difference. I want to be a voice for those children who don't have a voice ... I'm always looking for ways that I can use myself and use my life, use my money, use my time, use my energy ... What I'm interested in doing now is creating a lasting impact ... My efforts [are] going into schools because education is freedom." In 2007, Oprah dedicated $40 million to open The Oprah Winfrey Leadership Academy for Girls in South Africa. Oprah said, "When you educate a girl, you begin to change the face of a nation. The school is going to change the trajectory of their lives."

Jack Canfield

Cocreator of the Chicken Soup for the Soul *series of books and products, among the most successful lines in the self help arena.*

Jack Canfield (and his partner Mark Victor Hansen) used the principle of *Build the Castle First.* They envisioned their book, *Chicken Soup for the Soul,* topping the *New York Times* Bestsellers List. They cut out a copy of the list from the newspaper and modified it with their book at the top.

Mark Victor Hansen

Cocreator of the Chicken Soup for the Soul *series of books and products, among the most successful lines in the self help arena.*

Mark Victor Hansen's famous phrase is "Don't think it, ink it!" This is in line with the principle *Build the Castle First.* Also, Mark Victor Hansen uses principles of *Energize.* He listens to educational audio programs while he exercises.

Brian Tracy

Brian Tracy is a bestselling author and public speaker who has helped over 4 million people achieve their goals.

Brian Tracy used the principle of *Surround Yourself with the Compelling* as he raised himself from poverty. For example, he learned how to do real estate deals by reading every book on real estate available at the public library. Today, he still reads hundreds of books and magazine articles to keep his knowledge current and to increase his effectiveness.

Anthony Robbins

For the past three decades, Anthony Robbins has served as an advisor to leaders around the world as a recognized authority on the psychology of leadership, organizational turnaround, and peak performance.

Anthony Robbins used the principle of *Surround Yourself with the Compelling*. He approached top speaker/author Jim Rohn and asked to join Rohn's team. Rohn reportedly required him to purchase his success-system so that he could learn what he would be selling firsthand. As a teenager, Anthony went to a number of banks until he secured a loan for the purchase price. Anthony's persistence gained him Jim Rohn as a mentor for a significant part of his early business life.

Warren Buffet

Legendary investor often ranked among the wealthiest people in the world. His partnership with Bill Gates has resulted in the creation of the world's largest philanthropic foundation.

Warren Buffet uses the principle, *Surround Yourself with the Compelling*. He said, "It's better to hang out with people better than you. Pick out associates whose behavior is better than yours, and you'll drift in that direction." Journalist Larry Kanter described Warren Buffet's strategy, "Ignoring both macroeconomic trends and Wall Street fashions, [Warren Buffet] looks for undervalued companies with low overhead costs, high growth potential, strong market share, and low price-to-earnings ratios, and then waits for the rest of the world to catch up."

Donald Trump

Eminent real estate developer, casino mogul, reality TV host, and business celebrity.

Donald Trump uses the *Power of Alliances* (a portion of *Surround Yourself with the Compelling*). He teamed up with Mark Burnett for the hit television show *The Apprentice*. On an episode of *Larry King Live*, Donald Trump said, "Robert [Kiyosaki] wrote a book that was a tremendous success, [sold] like 30-some-odd million copies of *Rich Dad, Poor Dad*, and I wrote a book called *The Art of the Deal*, which was the biggest selling business book of all time,* and since then I've written a lot of other books, and they've all gone into being best-sellers, and we just wanted to join forces [to co-write the book *Why We Want You to Be Rich*]." Donald Trump also said, "I actually think the most important tip is [to] go into something that you love because you'll learn it ... more quickly than if you just don't like the subject matter."

Suze Orman

New York Times *number one bestselling author, known as "America's most trusted personal finance expert"*

Suze Orman uses the *Build the Castle First* principle. She said, "People first, then money, then things." She also said, "To choose [to be] rich is to make every penny count, every dollar count, every financial choice count." Also, "In all realms of life it takes courage to stretch your limits, express your power, and fulfill your potential ... it's no different in the financial realm." She added, "Courage is the ability to face danger, difficulty, uncertainty, or pain without being overcome by fear or being deflected from a chosen course of action." She wrote, "Truth Creates Money, Lies Destroy it."

....

* It appears this title actually belongs to Napoleon Hill's *Think and Grow Rich*, which had sold over 60 million copies (as of 2008) and continues to sell at a rate of a million copies annually.

Walt Disney

Legendary entertainment innovator in animation and motion pictures and the creator of the theme park.

Walt Disney originated the *Build the Castle First* idea. He also used the principle of *Surround Yourself with the Compelling.* To ensure that new members of his animation team would do great work, he set up an internal "university" so they would learn and excel. Walt said, "I have always had men working for me whose skills were greater than my own. I am an idea man." Walt also emphasized, "Everyone has been remarkably influenced by a book." This was certainly true for Walt in that he first learned animation from a book. Finally, he said, "Disneyland is a work of love. We didn't go into Disneyland just with the idea of making money."

> *Nothing can stop you when you*
> *use the B.E.S.T. principles!*

Conclusion to Part I

In Part I, we have covered important strategies based on these four principles:

         B – Build the Castle First

         E – Energize

         S – Surround Yourself with The Compelling

         T – Turn Around Your Moods

In Part II, we will delve further into proven methods of *Quick Breakthroughs for Your Success.*

I am grateful for this opportunity to work with you. Please know that living on the level of gratitude will *energize* you. It is part of the QuickBreakthrough Level.

Imagine how great you'll feel when you make breakthroughs in your life. Turn the page and you're on your way!

Part II

7

Quick Breakthroughs for Your Success

Introduction

W hat advantages will you have when you function at the QuickBreakthrough Level? You will experience success in:

- Job interviews
- Improving your own business
- Closing sales quickly
- Better business relationships
- Better personal relationships

The Einstein Factor Secret

> *You can never solve a problem on the*
> *level on which it was created.*

ALBERT EINSTEIN

As I mentioned earlier, the solution is to learn to shift to the QuickBreakthrough Level of perceiving, feeling, thinking, and acting. I call this the *Einstein Factor Secret.** *

> *Your hidden power is the ability to shift
> to the QuickBreakthrough Level.*

The empowered state of the QuickBreakthrough Level is one of heightened awareness and flexibility. When you are functioning on the QuickBreakthrough Level, you have the flow of:

- Intuition

- Cooperation

- Connection

- Creativity

- Integrity (wholeness)

- Excellent communication

- Effective action

At the QuickBreakthrough Level, you are free from distraction, pain, worry, limited thinking, judgments, and emotional baggage. You do *not* procrastinate (see Part II, Chapter 9: *Use Time-Leverage*).

••••••••••••••••••••••••••••••••

* Perhaps you've heard this notable quote before. The secret lies in the fact that the QuickBreakthrough Level of which Einstein spoke is one that we can willfully choose to elevate ourselves to. This is wholly in contrast to Einstein's implication that a breakthrough requires the enormous feat of a paradigm shift.

On the QuickBreakthrough Level, you have the full use of your resources and skills to gain the cooperation of other people.

We use the Q.U.I.C.K. Process:

> Q – Qualify
>
> U – Use Time-Leverage
>
> I – Intuit to Do It!
>
> C – Create (Don't Compete)
>
> K – Kindle Brand

Turn the page and you'll be on your way to gain the advantages of the QuickBreakthrough Level.

8

Qualify

How do you get on and stay on the QuickBreakthrough Level? You make effective choices.

When we learn to *qualify our thoughts* and choose which thoughts to focus on, we *double our productivity*. We also enjoy more moments feeling calm and fulfilled.

When you qualify your thoughts, you get these benefits:

- You avoid pain

- You avoid wasting time

- You create space for calmness, clarity, and feelings of fulfillment.

Princeton University's WordNet defines *qualify*: "pronounce fit or able." To qualify your thoughts, make a decision about whether a thought is fit or able to help you live in more capable ways.

Mahatma Gandhi said, "I will not let anyone walk through my mind with their dirty feet." This is the basis of qualifying our thoughts so that we avoid losing momentum, productivity, and feelings of accomplishment and fulfillment.

How to Qualify Your Thoughts

The moment you have a thought, use these three guidelines:

A principle: Don't engage in mischief.

A question: Is this a teaching moment?

A principle: Avoid a downward spiral.

The idea, *don't engage in mischief,* is to avoid making a situation worse. Marina has found that if she avoids giving her mother a direct conflicting reply (such as, "That's wrong. I want to do …") she avoids creating more uncomfortable feelings. Instead, Marina replies, "Maybe so …" when her mother voices an opinion. Marina does *not* engage in mischief.

A *teaching moment* occurs when someone is open to learning something from us. A teaching moment feels like a rare occasion, because many of us are obsessed with our own opinions and perceptions. I share with my audiences that it's rare for someone to come to us, saying, "You are a fount of wisdom! I am a sponge."

When there is *no* teaching moment, we avoid difficulty by *not* trying to teach a detail to someone. We avoid gushing advice. We focus on being in the moment, and often, we do more listening.

A *downward spiral* is a pattern of thoughts that takes you into a bad mood.

For Nadine, the pattern is like a reflexive reaction. Her roommate sets her up with a blind date, who is late. Nadine thinks, "Oh! He's late because he doesn't really care about me. He saw a photograph of me and he's not interested. In fact, he'll continue to treat me disrespectfully and …"

In a few moments of Nadine's downward spiral of thinking, she already sees their divorce, and they haven't gone on a first date!

An interviewer asked, "This idea, *qualify your thoughts*, sounds helpful. But what if I am really hurting? I notice that when I am really hurting, my thoughts tend to replay over and over."

"Yes," I replied. "That happens to many us on a number of occasions. It takes a process of learning to create forgiveness in our lives in order to help us break free from a downward spiral pattern of thoughts." Next, in response to the interviewer's question, I shared the following ideas from my book *Wake Up Your Spirit to Prosperity*:

"Viewing forgiveness as the big picture allows us to go through the process of letting go of our painful feelings.

Forgiveness is not pardon; it's seeing the big picture.

Marina experienced a huge disappointment. For months she helped her friend, Janet, organize a conference. Marina assumed that she would be rewarded with an opportunity to give a presentation at the event. Her speaking business was just starting, and she really needed a break. Marina had expressed to Janet her desire to give a speech.

At the last minute, Marina discovered that she had *not* been included on the conference agenda. This broke her heart. How could her friend be so unfair and cruel?

I guided Marina through the *Big Picture Forgiveness Process*. Using the four-step process, Marina began by acknowledging her personal truth, which was that she felt deeply hurt. She overcame her disappointment by expanding her perspective.

The Big Picture Forgiveness Process

Step 1: Acknowledge the pain. Marina said, "I'm really disappointed and hurt that Janet didn't give me the opportunity to serve her audience – especially after the help I gave her with the conference preparation."

Step 2: Take care of yourself. Marina treated herself with warm baths, relaxing music, and time to write in her journal. She also processed her feelings as we talked through the situation.

Step 3: Examine the situation to gain objectivity from the perspective of a metaphorical helicopter. In time, Marina was able to say, "Janet didn't include me on her list because she was only including speakers who already had a long list of fans. Janet was only focused on making her conference a success. I understand that. But I still feel that she could have included me in some way. Since it was a spiritual conference, perhaps I could have led the prayer at dinnertime."

Step 4: Become the hero of your own story. Marina eventually said, "Janet's not including me in the conference became a warning sign that I need to change my perspective. I need to have faith that God will provide me with other opportunities. Also, I need to *step up my participation.* I need to intensify my focus. I want to devote more time to marketing my speaking career. I can't control what others do, but I can make better choices for myself."

~~~~~~~~~~~~~~~

Months later, Marina still talks to Janet on the telephone from time to time. Marina's healthy approach to forgiveness has saved a friendship, and perhaps opened the door for her friendship with Janet to deepen over time. The good news is Marina is now free of her painful feelings. Her time and energy have been set free, too."

> *When you select some of the letters*
> *from forgiveness, you get* free.

This is the idea behind *qualify your thoughts*: Respond to any negative thought (such as, "He's late, and that means he'll always be disrespectful toward me") with these three thoughts:

1. Don't engage in mischief.

2. Is this a teaching moment?

3. Avoid a downward spiral.

The next step is to let the negative thought flow away as if it were on a river. This can be as simple as playing a favorite CD and having your thoughts drift in a positive direction. In other situations, the *Big Picture Forgiveness Process* will prove helpful.

Principle:

Qualify your thoughts and avoid downward spirals.

Power Question:

What thought triggers a downward spiral, and how can you replace that thought?

9

Use Time-Leverage

Ever feel that your time management process has failed you? Ever write something on your to-do list then procrastinate and move the task to the next day? And then to the day after that?

You don't need time management.
You need Time-Leverage!

Leverage is using little effort for big results. Picture using a branch with a small rock as a fulcrum – and moving a boulder! That's leverage.

Time-Leverage™ is the process of reducing resistance and going into action quickly with minimal energy. In this way, Time-Leverage provides the Easethrough™ that I mentioned in Part I, Chapter 1. With Time-Leverage, you neutralize your own resistance, which can create procrastination.

For many readers, this section serves as the most valuable part of this book. Why? Because Time-Leverage is an essential part of your hidden power.

> *Your hidden power is the ability*
> *to shift to the QuickBreakthrough Level.*

Using Time-Leverage, we shift away from pain and the anticipation of pain, which researchers note are sources of procrastination.* The anguish of procrastination keeps us off the QuickBreakthrough Level.

Procrastination can also be the result of fear and feeling ambivalence. Now, Dr. Elayne Savage talks about overcoming ambivalence so you can move forward.

Get Out Of Your Own Way!
Overcoming ambivalence & the fears that hold you back

ELAYNE SAVAGE, PHD

Attaining personal and professional goals involves putting yourself 'out there'. However, by its nature this opens you up to the possibility of rejection.

••••••••••••••••••••••••••••••

* Dr. Kevin P. Austin, a psychologist and director of the Student Counseling Services at California Institute of Technology notes, "For some students, each time they approach a task they consider important, the feelings of being pressured to do a perfect job come up [accompanied by] a sense of the inevitability of failure ... What if you started early, tried your best, and then you could be judged fairly for what you are capable of?"

And rejection hurts.

Fear of Rejection is huge, yet it doesn't exist alone. It is part of something bigger. I call it 'The Fear Team': Fear of Rejection's evil twin, the Fear of Failure. Joined by Fear of Judgments and Criticism, Fear of Success and Fear of Being Visible. And let's not forget the sneaky one that causes so much trouble … Fear of Disappointment.

Make no mistake about it, though. Fear of Rejection is the team leader, the most strident voice. Fear of Rejection is the foundation for all the other Fears.

Whenever I attempt to put myself 'out there', I notice other voices enter into the mix. And a shouting match takes place in my head:

> "I can make a difference!" "Says who!"
> "I can!" "You can't!"
> "I will." "You won't."
> "I'm going to try." "Why bother?"
> Opposing voices swirl around. "You can't do it! You can't
>   do it!" answered by "Yes, I can! Yes, I can!"

It's a struggle to recognize options through the haze. I feel trapped. I get anxious. Sometimes I freeze up. Do you, too, feel this way? Stuck? Unable to make choices? Powerless to act? Do you, too, become immobilized?

The Whispers and Roars of Ambivalence

Let's try to sort it out. We can start by looking at that exhausting tug-of-war between the whispers and roars of the voices.

This is ambivalence.

For some folks the word "ambivalence" means "love and hate" or "good and bad." But there are actually many kinds of ambivalent feelings and thoughts. Ambivalence is the presence of simultaneously conflicting feelings, ideas, or wishes competing with each other. And a bit of it is natural to all of us.

It's a tip-off you're ambivalent when you experience uncomfortable inner conflict and can't make a decision. You feel stuck, like you're straddling a fence.

You may find yourself experiencing a wide-range of ambivalent personal and professional situations:

- Having trouble deciding which mail (or papers or files or clothes) to keep and which to toss

- Wanting to spend time with someone, and at the same time wanting time for yourself

- Wanting a romantic relationship, yet not being quite ready to make a commitment

- Wanting connectedness but needing separateness and personal space

- Wanting a promotion or special project, yet dreading the added work hours it would require

- Having trouble making up your mind about which gift or card to buy You may even end up avoiding more anxiety by buying nothing

The Seeds of Ambivalence

Ambivalence is influenced by messages we hear in our early years, often in the form of admonitions from parents, teachers, or peers:

- "You're such a dreamer."
- "What makes you think you can do that?"
- "Who do you think you are?"

Warnings like these are rejecting messages. They discount, dismiss, and diminish. Over time we begin to interpret these warnings as "Be careful. You could fail." You can see how cautions like these are not conducive to taking risks, to putting yourself out there.

And for many of us, putting ourselves out there brings up a myriad of fears. For some of us it may be Fear of Rejection or Failure or Success. For others it may be Fear of Visibility or Disappointment. It may be all of these.

Uncertainty, Confusion, Anxiety

When two internal voices start skirmishing with one another this creates conflict that leads to uncertainty and confusion.

The confusion creates anxiety. The anxiety can cause us to freeze up and become immobilized. Surely it's not productive.

You can see how much energy it takes to deal with these conflicting voices. Wouldn't you like to make the choice to put your energy elsewhere?

Five Tips for Taming Ambivalence

By moving past the ambivalence, it's possible to leave space for making choices.

Here's how.

1. Give both voices a chance to be heard. Whenever you're listening to only one voice you are, in effect, rejecting the other.

   You might even encourage the voices to talk to each other. Out loud. Writing to each other works, too. Then read it out loud.

   In other words, you'll be giving voice to both sides of the ambivalence. You'll be honoring both voices.

   One way to do this is to make two lists: a 'What I Have to Gain' list and a 'What I Have to Lose' list.

2. It's probably some type of Fear immobilizing you. You can begin to move forward by naming it. Is it Fear of Rejection? Of Failure? Of Success? Of being Visible? Of Disappointment? Of Judgment?

   Try these steps, First name the Fear to yourself. Next, write it down. Then say it out loud. Hearing yourself say it allows you to see it differently and to recognize possible options.

   (By the way, these fears are not only attached to your early experiences. Admonitions and family messages of Fear are often passed down from generation to generation.)

3. Next approach the Fear with some detachment. I call it 'walking alongside yourself.' This means stepping back enough to recognize when you may be starting down that old path of doubt and fear. When you can take some distance from your emotional tug-of-war you can create choices.

4. Then, ask yourself, "Do I really want to continue down this path?

   Remind yourself: "I could retrace my steps and make the choice to back up to the fork in the road. I can go down a different road."

5. You can learn more about your own early messages by asking yourself a few questions:

   If I put myself "out there" it would mean _____?

   If I fail, it would mean _____?

   If I succeed, it would mean _____?

   Might I feel disloyal to someone?_____?

   Who would that be? _____?

   If I feel too visible what might happen?_____?

Creating Space to Make Choices

Hearing yourself think out loud allows the space you need to recognize your options.

Sometimes it's helpful to have someone else to talk to – especially someone who is professionally skilled in guiding you through this process.

Putting your confusion into words gives it a container and creates definition. This allows enough space for choices to emerge.

And it allows you the space to move forward.

Dr. Elayne Savage is The Queen of Rejection,® communication coach, consultant, and speaker. She helps people not take rejection so personally. Elayne is the author of two books published in nine languages, *Don't Take It Personally! The Art of Dealing with Rejection* and *Breathing Room – Creating Space to Be a Couple* (New Harbinger). Her website www.QueenofRejection.com is loaded with rejection tips and articles. Her e-letter 'Tips from The Queen of Rejection' ® can be found at http://queenofrejection.typepad.com/tips/

You can reach Elayne at (510) 540-6230 or elayne@QueenofRejecton.com

Dr. Elayne encourages us to move past ambivalence and create space to make new choices.

Shift to an Empowered State of Being

Time-Leverage™ is better than standard time management. Time-Leverage uses your emotions as a fulcrum. That's how Time-Leverage gets you into action. Standard time management, using only a written list, does not give a person the energy to get into action.

*If you're not using Time-Leverage,
you're working too hard and too long.*

Over the years, I have developed the Science of Emotional Leverage™. My focus has been to help people overcome their stuck-points formed by standard time management. The idea is to empower you to gain access to your natural brilliance and take effective action without hesitation.

Time-Leverage Doubles Your Productivity

Imagine that you can avoid procrastination. Then imagine that you can accomplish work based on your natural brilliance. Sounds terrific, yes? Our solution is to use the G.O.—N.O.W. Process that I devised for my audio program, *Power Time Management: More Time, Less Stress and Zero Procrastination.*

To overcome procrastination, we use the G.O.—N.O.W. Process:

> G – Get the pain out
>
> O – Offer fun
>
> N – Nurture rewards
>
> O – Open the pain valve
>
> W – Wrangle schedules

Get the Pain Out

Emotional Leverage™ is using your emotional buttons to move yourself to action. Many people procrastinate to avoid

G
O
.
N
O
W

anticipated pain. The strategy is to get the pain out of the situation and eliminate hesitation. That's when you experience an Easethrough. If you procrastinate writing because you hate facing a blank screen, call a friend and talk about the report you intend to write. Record your side of the conversation. Then type up your comments. In this way, you eliminate the pain of facing a blank screen. All you have to do is type your recording, and you will have made a good start. I call this process the *Easy Part Start*. Momentum breeds momentum. Start with an easy part.

Offer Fun

Use strategy and inject fun into your difficult task. Imagine that to *offer fun* is to *offer a solution to the procrastination problem*. You offer fun to your inner child to get the burst of energy you desire. The inner child is that part of you that feels small and vulnerable and wants to enjoy fun.

Our solution is to add something enjoyable to your work process. For example, if you don't like doing tax paperwork, play your favorite music. Or have a barn-raising event. In the Amish community, the townspeople gather and build a barn together; this is called barn-raising. In the same way, you can work in parallel with a friend on your respective tax paperwork. Then you can take breaks together. Use my process, *Keep Score and Achieve More.* Have a friendly contest counting the number of receipts each person logs in a personal spreadsheet. Use these questions:

- How can I do this and enjoy the process?
- How can I happily achieve?

"Offer fun" Also Refers to Your Thinking Style

A convergent thinking-style person is methodical and feels comfortable concentrating for long periods of time. A divergent thinker has a mind that jumps around; meanwhile, surprising creative links pop up.

If you are a divergent thinking-style person, don't force yourself to start at the beginning of a report. Set up your section headings and bounce around. Use a divide-and-conquer approach. Make sure to have a methodical or convergent friend or co-worker look at a rough draft. Seeing the person's corrections or comments (like "more needed here") helps you feel that you're participating in a dialogue. You can avoid feeling that you're stuck in a cave while being forced to concentrate.

"Offer Fun" Relates to Input Styles

At one point, I discovered that I was avoiding reading certain time management books. This was due to my dislike of getting input by reading dry material about this subject. Reading those particular books was not fun at the time. So I switched to listening to audio CDs while using a cross-country skiing exercise machine. When it came to dry text, my preferred input style was auditory.

"Offer Fun" Focuses on Entrainment

To *entrain* is to synchronize with the rhythm of something in your environment. Women in the same household find that their monthly cycles entrain with each other. To create fun, set up your time so that you entrain with something enjoyable like your favorite music. Sometimes, I play the theme music from *Indiana Jones: The Raiders of the Lost Ark* to energize myself to handle paperwork.

Think of Time-Delight

Time-Delight is a takeoff on my concept of *Customer-Delight,** which is based on giving something extra and surprising. Make sure that your schedule includes fun and delight to offset fatigue-generating thoughts, such as, "I have to do this."

Make a Shift for Renewal

Imagine feeling comfortable as if you were luxuriating in a hot, soothing bath. Now, imagine that you hear soothing music that makes calm, peaceful energy flow through you. You smell the delightful fragrance of an aroma-therapy candle.

• •

* In the current world of cut-throat pricing, satisfied customers are not necessarily loyal customers. In light of this, effective salespeople use my Customer Delight principle to go beyond mere customer satisfaction, by giving something extra and surprising. For additional information about the Customer Delight principle, refer to my audio program *Double Your Sales in Half the Time.* Available at www.TomSuperCoach.com.

The peaceful feelings I describe are available to you. Some people talk of meditation or devoting time for prayer. As the author of *Wake Up Your Spirit to Prosperity* and *Wake Up Your Spirit to Prosperity for Couples*, and as a college instructor of comparative religion, I know that people find renewal when they participate in activities that renew the spirit. I invite you to include spiritual activities in your life.

During one of my meditative, quiet times I experienced a place of no striving, no strain, and no goal-obsession. When I returned to my usual focus, I felt renewed and I realized that I can enjoy both the peace of a quiet time and then return to the thrill of making dreams come true.

Nurture Rewards

According to the dictionary, *to nurture* is "to promote the development of." To nurture rewards is to develop your system of rewarding yourself. Rewards work. When my father wanted me to learn to swim, he provided rewards. Now, I provide my own rewards, or self-rewards. Think of this as a bonus. What bonus or reward is so enticing that it will enable you to do an onerous task?

Nurture rewards reminds you to nurture your inner child, the source of your energy. If you don't take care of your inner child, you end up with an inner rebel who feels fatigue or acts in some self-destructive manner.

Open your journal and write the question: "Inner child, how can I take better care of you right now?" Then write your answers quickly without censoring them. You may find yourself seeing silly movies or playing Frisbee or taking a Sunday afternoon off to soak in a hot bath. Good! You'll be amazed by your energy and efficiency on Monday.

My clients also mention these rewards:

- Going to a favorite restaurant
- Attending a symphony performance
- Devoting time in one's garden
- Playing with a grandchild
- Browsing in a bookstore

Give yourself the reward of a preview of the terrific feelings and experiences you will have when the task is done. A writer can envision autographing books at book signings. She can envision making so much money from writing that she says goodbye to her onerous day job. She can envision going on vacations around the world and receiving letters of gratitude, proclaiming how her book has improved lives. Energize yourself by recording an "audio commercial" that is your description of your new terrific life. Each morning, as you brush your teeth, you can replay your audio commercial. Or make a video recording if a video commercial is more compelling.

Open the Pain Valve

Researchers show that people will do more to avoid pain than   G
to gain joy.* When that's true, imagine turning up the pain – or   O
open the *pain valve*. My client, Pat, procrastinated visiting the   •
computer repair shop to have a hard drive reformatted, because   N
she had to back up all files before bringing the computer in. I   **o**
advised her to imagine the pain caused by this situation. Pat   w
reported that she hated hearing her father's voice saying, "We
buy you a computer, and you just let it sit!" She took action
because she did not want to hear the same hurtful words and
tone from her father. This is the second form of Emotional
Leverage™: you use pain as your button to take action.

Wrangle Schedules

In feature films, a horse wrangler ensures that the horse   G
does what it needs to do at the right time. When you wrangle   O
schedules, you overcome a prevalent problem.   •

People often procrastinate because they do *not* have a viable   N
plan. Many people stop working because they have made their   O
plan too formidable and intimidating. With the *Power-Three*   w

....

* Kevin Hogan, bestselling author, consultant, and corporate trainer, wrote:
"Decades of scientific research clearly show that people are more motivated
by pain than by pleasure. In fact, pain is approximately 2.5 times more of a
motivator than pleasure is. What this means is that you not only will paint
a picture of a vivid wonderful future for your customer, but you must also
find their current wounds (pain) and heal them."

Action Plan, I guide my clients to identify 3 levels of activity: (1) easy, (2) stretch, and (3) over-stretch.

For example, Sandra starts her own business, but she lacks sales experience. I ask her what prospect-calling schedule would be easy. She says one call a day for a total of five calls per week. Ultimately, we set up two to ten calls in a day with a total of 10 per week for the first five weeks. Each week, she uses a "star" sticker. When she has five stars pinned on her bulletin board, she gets a new music CD. We set up a schedule with a bit of a stretch, which is at level 2 of the *Power-Three Action Plan*.

Second, Sandra needs an immediate morale boost in the form of an *Immediate Victory*, or I.V. During a hospital stay, a patient gains nutrients through an I.V. unit. Similarly, the I.V., or Immediate Victory, is the nutrient for your morale. Sandra's Immediate Victory was a coffee get-together with a friend within 4 hours of completing her first two phone calls.

Third, Sandra needs to *make it a game she can win.* That's why we've started her client-prospecting process gradually. She needs immediate victories. Sandra also uses a wall chart to log her activities. She learns to *keep score and achieve more.*

As human beings, we naturally like games related to leisure time. For millions of people, video games are a compelling activity. Why? Video games provide these results:

- Immediate feedback (your score)
- An opportunity to get better at the task
- A world in which the player has a degree of control

We can use the process of a game to *energize* you. Remember the old phrase: No one would go bowling if they couldn't see the pins drop. How can you show your progress to someone who cares about you and who is important to you? Use a *Moment of Appreciation*. That's when you go to a friend, say "I need of moment of appreciation" and recount what you did well. You bask in a moment of glory and appreciation. This process is like hearing a circus orchestra play TA-DAH while trapeze artists take a bow. Make sure that your schedule flows on the levels of easy and stretch. Avoid "over-stretching." Make sure that you begin with an I.V., an *Immediate Victory*. Reward yourself!

People procrastinate for two major reasons: (1) to avoid pain and (2) to duck the fear of making mistakes. At various times, you may not know how to handle a big project. Use the G.O.— N.O.W. Process to create a *Power-Three Action Plan*. Avoid the "over-stretch" level. Finally, reward yourself as you create your success, step-by-step and day-by-day.

Questions to Get Unstuck Fast

TOM MARCOUX

Imagine that you can quickly shift from a disempowering mood that creates procrastination. Would you get more done? Would you feel better?

Yes!

How can you make that shift quickly? Through questions. Near the beginning of this book, I mentioned the Secret of Real Power: questions, Emotional Charge, and intuition.

Below are powerful questions.* Write your answers in your journal to create powerful results in your life.

Get the Pain Out

What hurts about the task at hand? How can you get the pain out? Can you get help? Can you listen to music? Can you change your environment? Can you make phone calls from a different room? Can you record your thoughts on an audio recorder and pay your nephew to type your words on a computer? Can you trade services with a friend? Can you hire an expert, such as a professional editor?

Offer Fun

How can you make the process fun? Can you do this with a friend? Can you work on taxes paperwork together in the same room? Can you ask your spouse to work with you for the first 15 minutes? Can you use a laptop computer on your back porch and enjoy the outdoors?

Nurture Rewards

What bonus or compelling reward would entice you to start now? How can you break down the project into a small step with a great reward attached to it?

• •

* These questions were first revealed in my audio program *Power Time Management: More Time, Less Stress, and Zero Procrastination*, in which I coach you in real-time to get unstuck and to stop procrastinating.

Open the pain valve

Researchers show that many people will do more to avoid pain than to gain joy.* So get a preview of the pain you will suffer if you do not break this procrastination. Don't hold back! Write it down! What terrible thing would happen if you didn't do this task? What big regret will you feel if you don't get started? If at 80 years old, you were to find yourself sitting in a rocking chair and you hadn't done this task (such as writing a book or making a small digital movie), how bad would you feel? Would you feel ashamed? Would you feel that you missed a chance for a fulfilling life?

Wrangle schedules

Do you have a viable, encouraging plan? Do you need to get more information? Are you confused, and do you not know how to begin? Who can help you? Add a schedule to get help (or input) to the start of your plan. Use a *Power-Three Action* Plan. Identify the 3 levels of activity: (1) easy, (2) stretch, and (3) over-stretch. Would 20 minutes a day be easy? Would one hour a day be a stretch? Would 30 minutes in the morning and 30 minutes in the afternoon be easy? How are you going to log your progress? How are you going to make it a game you can win? Remember, keep score and achieve more.

• •

* "Principle 2: People will usually do more to avoid pain than to gain pleasure. Although it's more inspirational to focus on helping your prospect achieve their dreams, it's a fact that, for most people, pain is a more powerful motivator than pleasure. Achieving pleasure is optional, avoiding pain is non-negotiable. Examples? Ninety percent of smokers stopped smoking only after a serious heart attack or cancer diagnosis." David C. Miller, MS, PCC, professional business coach.

I have found that when I ask effective questions, both radio show callers and my clients discover how to gain more with their time – more money, more love, and more fulfillment. In fact, because of my questions, I am called the Time-Leverage Detective.

The Principles of Time-Leverage™

Now that we have discussed the G.O.—N.O.W. Process, let's look at some other principles of *Time-Leverage*. Time-Leverage provides you these benefits:

- Get more done
- Stop procrastinating
- Eliminate guilt
- Feel better!

The phrase time management is misguided. We don't manage time. We learn to make effective choices. We learn to make choices and take action that give us leverage: *the most benefit for the least effort.*

What do you want in relation to your time management? My clients have told me: more time, less stress, and zero procrastination. Employers and the self-employed want more productivity in less time. Here's the problem: with a day planner system or the latest book on time management, many of us get excited for two weeks and then backslide into our old habits.

Instead, let's use the Science of Emotional Leverage™ to break this cycle. Here's the other problem: many people are natural turtles trying to become racehorses; or owls attempting to be lions. *Stop fighting yourself.* Use your natural tendencies to your best advantage.

We use the T.I.M.E. Process:

> T – Target
> I – Intensify
> M – Minimize
> E – Expect

Target

Target *Effort Goals.* Effort Goals are targets that are in your control. For example, if you want to increase sales, you control how many phone calls you make. You can have an Effort Goal of making five more phone calls per day than you already make. On the other hand, a *Result Goal* would aim for one extra customer per week.

Unfortunately, many people only focus on Result Goals. A Result Goal depends on many things: the mood of the person you are calling, the weather, the state of the market and more. Sometimes, we do everything right and still don't gain the result we desire.

The distinction between Effort Goals and Result Goals helps us improve personal productivity and keep up our morale.

Effort Goals always make you feel good, because they are what you can control. Remember that you can always feel proud yourself when you complete your Effort Goals.

Effort Goals grow naturally from your values; that is, what is most important to you. To *target* your values, write the answer to the following questions in your personal journal:

- What is most important in your life?

- What's working in your life?

- What's not working in your life?

- What is working in your time management?

- How is your time management not working?

- In which areas do you procrastinate?

- What finally breaks the procrastination?

- How can you create closeness with people who are important to you?

- To feel good about your life, what has to happen?

- To feel good about yourself, what has to happen?

If you were talking to the genie of *Aladdin*, what would you wish for? If you could have or do anything you wanted (even if it required five years in real time), what would you wish for? You must vocalize this. You cannot hit a vague target!

To help my clients complete their Effort Goals, I coach them to use a *Self-Leadership Chart*™. On the chart, with a grid labeled Monday through Sunday, they place their vital daily tasks. To keep their vital tasks in mind, they check the chart daily.

Self-Leadership Chart™							
Effort Goal (E) or Result Goal (R)	*Mon*	*Tues*	*Wed*	*Thu*	*Fri*	*Sat*	*Sun*
Check this chart (E)	√	√	√	√	√	√	√
Exercise (E)	√		√	√	√		
5 phone calls per day (E)	√	√	√	√			
20 minutes quiet time (E)	√	√	√			√	√
Gain one extra customer per week (R)					√		

The Self-Leadership Chart™ helps you overcome backsliding and replace undesired behavior.

Do you see how the Self-Leadership Chart™ gives you credit for any desired action that you accomplish? This is especially helpful since backsliding tends to occur when people start to change their personal behavior. I also help clients prepare for backsliding. Instead of calling it "failing," we call it "hesitating." For example, if Sonia is disappointed because she fails to go to the gym one day out of three, she can *shift her perception*. She is *not* failing! She has still succeeded in increasing her good behavior by 66.7%. Well done!

The effective strategy is to *inoculate oneself for backsliding*. My clients construct two or three presets so they can immediately get back on the horse. If Sonia misses a session at the gym, she can take a 20-minute walk in her neighborhood or ride her stationary bicycle while watching television. Using a *backup plan*, Sonia is still making progress.

Researchers emphasize that when a memory is formed, neural pathways are set in the brain.* In formulating my Science of Emotional Leverage™, I noted two effective processes. One is letting the neural pathway fade from disuse. The plan is to drop self-accusation and instead use the label *hesitation*. The other process is *replacing undesired behavior.* Instead of reaching for a can of regular soda (full of sugar and calories), Sonia can drink water with a squeeze of lemon for flavor. Replacing a behavior and replacing a neural pathway are effective methods for improving your life. Then *nothing can stop you!*

Intensify

Intensify customization. That is, do things that work for you. Researchers note that people often procrastinate because they anticipate pain or inconvenience.** When a day planner becomes inconvenient or unwieldy, many of us stop using the it.

• •

* "Our data strongly suggest that the hippocampal neural pathway called the tri-synaptic pathway, or TSP, plays a crucial role in quickly forming memories when encountering new events and episodes in day-to-day life," reported Susumu Tonegawa and fellow researchers at the Picower Institute for Learning and Memory at MIT. They reported on a revolutionary method for visualizing how bypassing a major memory-forming circuit in the brain affected learning and memory in mice. ScienceDaily.com, "New Tool Probes Brain Circuits: Method Applied to Learning and Memory Pathway," Jan. 31, 2008.

** Timothy A. Pychyl, PhD, an associate professor of psychology at Carleton University in Ottawa, wrote "Procrastination is associated with active attempts to regulate the immediate mood (*e.g.*, "Giving in to feel good") and to protect or enhance self-concept."

Instead, we must customize our day-planning system to make it easy to use and to minimize our time involved.

On the other hand, most day-planning training pushes you to do it *its* way, according to *its* system. It works better when I help a client discover his or her own way. For example, some day planning training systems dictate that everything should be placed in the day planner. But my day planner became so heavy that I did not feel like opening the planner or even holding it.

My solution was each night before sleep, I would write on a 3x5-inch card my *Top Six Targets* for the next day. That cleared my mind and also gave me efficient marching orders for the next morning. In this way, I customized my day planning system and avoided the discomfort of a heavy day planner. Other people use a Palm Pilot or another personal digital assistant, which is light and convenient for them.

Minimize

Minimize time-wasters. Bad habits waste your time; certain co-workers waste your time, too. You neutralize these time-wasters with *replacement behaviors*. For TV channel surfing, set a timer. If you happen upon a good program, start your VCR or digital recorder. Then, you will get the sleep you need.

To deal with that talkative co-worker, get up from your desk and say pleasantly, "Great talking with you, Sam. Well, I've got to get back to work."

Finally, I coach my clients in ways to say no effectively and graciously. One method is to say, "I'll have to say no at this time.

My plate is full. Thanks for thinking of me. Perhaps I can help you brainstorm to figure out who can help you with that."

Expect

T

I

M

E

When I say "expect," I'm referring to a process I call *Expectation Management.*

> *Expectation Management is a process of arranging your schedule so that you can experience fulfillment and avoid disappointment.*

For some people, a day planner is a guilt-producing device. If we write 30 tasks on a single day planner page, we might be setting ourselves up to feel guilty if we fail to complete them in one day!

Instead, using Expectation Management, write down a list of your daily *Top Six Targets* (tasks) in 30 seconds. Your top six targets are tasks that you think of in response to the following questions:

1. What is the most productive thing for me to do now?

2. What is the most profitable thing for me to do now?

3. What will benefit my life most when I do it today?

4. How can I take better care of myself now?

5. Which seeds do I need to plant today that will blossom into big gains in my life?

In presentations to audiences, I say, "Your top six targets – two for you, two for work, and two for family."

> *Expectation Management is also about*
> *managing the expectations of people*
> *who ask or demand things of you.*

For example, Joseph asks Jenny, "When can you get the Ari-7 Report done?" Jenny knows from experience that completing the Ari-7 Report usually takes her 3 hours. She replies, "If nothing surprising pops up, I can have it on your desk at 4 p.m." She gives herself 3 extra hours as a cushion. In this way, she *manages Joseph's expectations.*

Richard Carlson, author of the *Don't Sweat the Small Stuff* series wrote, "make allowances for incompetence." This is a way to manage your own expectations. When you expect incompetence, you compensate for possible errors created by other people. For example, save a copy of every check you send to vendors in case the post office or vendor loses your mail. In this way, you take proactive measures related to Expectation Management, and you make your life easier.

~~~~~~~~~~~~~~~~~~

In this chapter we have focused on Time-Leverage. We have looked at various ways that you can take action and shift yourself into an empowered state. Such an empowered state can help you double your productivity.

Principle:

Shift to an empowered state by getting the pain out.

Power Question:

Note a disempowered state that you fall into and what triggers it. How can you use the G.O.—N.O.W. Process to shift to an empowered state and to take action?

10

Intuit to Do It!

What if you were on the fast track to wealth? This chapter includes *Secrets for Sudden Profits*.

On the QuickBreakthrough Level, our intuition* gives us an edge in business and personal relationships. Albert Einstein said, "The only real valuable thing is intuition." We notice that we often do not have time to go through all the data that's available to us.

> *Intuition allows you to perceive your environment more clearly and broadly so that you are better equipped to respond to it.*
>
> LAURA DAY

• •

*One of my clients asked me, "How do I know the difference between my intuition and some fearful inner voice that is based on childhood conditioning?" I responded, "Fear often calls upon us to contract or close down. Fear often says, 'Don't do that, you might get hurt!' A number of authors (including Laura Day) note that intuition is the call for expansion. It's the voice of 'Try this. You may leap to a higher level.'"

Author John Naisbitt wrote, "Intuition becomes increasingly valuable in the new information society precisely because there is so much data."

We need to target the most important information. How do we know where to look and what to focus on? Intuition helps a lot.

Mary Kay Ash, founder of Mary Kay Cosmetics, wrote, "It was not extensive market surveys or demographic studies that created the pink Cadillac [her way to motivate consultants to excel], just [my] pure and simple woman's intuition."

Accessing your intuition gets you
access to sudden profits.

Imagine the moment someone realized that profit was available by using the sawdust in a mill to make pressboard! A similar thing happened when a man helped Ben and Jerry's ice cream company solve their problem of what to do with the waste from ice cream production. The solution? Provide it to local farmers to feed their pigs.

To activate your intuition, we take three steps.

3 Steps for Your Intuition

When you master these steps, you will gain the benefits of power, fulfillment and saving time. The whole idea is to shift to the QuickBreakthrough Level. This gets you away from the pattern of working harder and longer. Using intuition, you can discover the right things that will catapult your success as opposed to mediocre things that keep you on the hamster wheel.

Step 1: Make Space for Your Intuition

There are numerous times when we don't know exactly what the best course of action is. When possible, delay your decision making for some time, so that your intuition can work on the problem.

For example, late at night, if my sweetheart asks me, "Should we go to that event?" I reply, "If I answer now, I'll say 'no' because I'm tired. How about if we talk about this tomorrow?" In this way, I give my intuition time and space to work on the question, and often, I awaken with the answer.

Years ago, I had a tough career decision to make. At the time I was working as an operations analyst at a bank, and a position with another department came up. I felt torn by the pro's and con's of the decision. It looked like good money and job security. But I had a feeling that I was missing something. I took out a sheet of paper and wrote "Pro" on the left side and "Con" on the right side. I filled out the left side with nine "pro's" for taking the job. But then, on just the third "con," it was as if the words leapt up from the paper. My intuition spoke loudly and I chose to decline the position. I have always been happy with that decision.

Step 2: Inform Your Intuition

When you have a complicated problem, it helps to read about related topics, do an Internet search, and talk with appropriate people.

The intuitive leap occurs when you have effectively informed your intuition.

Let your intuition make surprising connections.

Related to this, Konosuke Matsushita said, "No matter how deep a study you make, what you really have to rely on is your own intuition and when it comes down to it, you really don't know what's going to happen until you do it."

Step 3: Ask Your Intuition!

With my clients, I emphasize the following:

The answer is in the question.
Ask better questions.
What am I learning here?
How can we make this better?

Write down your question before you go to sleep. Also, write down that you are asking your intuition and/or Higher Power to help you receive the best answer when you awaken.

A number of effective managers and CEOs take a power-nap; that is, they sleep for about 20 minutes at some point during the day. This is another example of recharging and making space for one's intuition to operate.

Use Power-4 Questions to Activate Your Intuition

These questions are designed to help you get the answers you need. Questions stimulate your thoughts and feelings and disrupt unproductive trances. This process takes you from a distracted state to one where you have enhanced access to inner resources, including intuition.*

Here are sample answers from one of my clients.

What is your highest leverage?

"Get my self-published book on Amazon.com."

What is the bottleneck?

"Get a bar code. I heard that it costs hundreds of dollars."

How much money? What are other methods?

"I'll need to find out via the Internet. But I heard that one company will provide a bar code for one book for around $100. I'll need to verify that."

Can someone else do it?

"I'm glad you mentioned this. I don't like doing this kind of work, and I'm afraid I'll make a mistake. But a good friend of mine is looking into this for his own book.

••••••••••••••••••••••••••••••

* "Your mind has what you might call an *Automatic Search Function*, which means that when you ask yourself a question, your mind automatically begins to search for an answer. (Psychologists have referred to this function of the human brain as the *embedded presupposition factor*.)," wrote Noah St. John. Asking questions will elicit feelings you were not previously conscious of. Questions gain access to your intuition, which lies hidden beneath the surface, in a method similar to a light shining down a well.

> *Perhaps, we can do a trade. I'll offer to make him a great dinner and take him to a movie."*

About Question 2: A bottleneck refers to the one thing that stops or impedes progress. (In a bottleneck, the passage is constricted, so little or nothing can get past.) Knowing the bottleneck is important. It guides you to solve what is critical to your situation.

More Powerful Thoughts on the Value of Intuition

> *You have to leave your city of comfort and go into the wilderness of your intuition. What you'll discover will be wonderful. What you'll discover is yourself.*

ALAN ALDA

> *Intuition is the supra-logic that cuts out all the routine processes of thought and leaps straight from the problem to the answer.*

ROBERT GRAVES

> *Walt Disney had a marvelous intuition. And because he understood people very well, liked them, and had great respect for people, there was nothing cynical about Walt.*

JOHN HENCH
member of Walt Disney's team

It is always with excitement that I wake up in the morning wondering what my intuition will toss up to me, like gifts from the sea. I work with it and rely on it. It's my partner.

JONAS SALK
discoverer of the first effective polio vaccine

Faith is a passionate intuition.

WILLIAM WORDSWORTH

Ten Secrets for Sudden Profits

Secret 1: Stop Trading Time for Money

Whether you make $8 or $300 per hour, you will see a real limit. When you stop trading time for money, you have created streams of income that automatically bring you wealth. For example, while writing this book, I would occasionally check my Web sites and find that orders had come for my previous books and CDs.

My clients who learn from my programs like *Online Secrets to Build Your Brand* and *Make Money through Products Power* literally make money while they sleep. Imagine your excitement: you can do the work *once* and continue to gain money over and over again. If you feel that you're not a "writer," you can use an audio recorder, have a niece type up your words, and have an editor shape the project. This works! I know, because years ago I served as a ghostwriter for a millionaire. The person had a bestselling book that sold around 1.4 million copies. Apparently, he hadn't written that book either.

Some people get stuck by the thought: "Well, a millionaire can afford an editor." My client, Celia, hired a friend for just $11 per hour (for a total of $66) to edit her small book. Remember: *many things are possible.*

Scott Turow, author of a number of bestselling books, wrote *Presumed Innocent* while riding the train to his job as an attorney. He found a way to do both: work at his regular job and create a source of additional income.

Secret 2: Ask Your Intuition Wealth-Generating Questions

Jack Canfield asked his intuition (his process was to ask God) for titles for bestselling books before he went to bed. Once when he did this, he woke up around 3:30 a.m. with 22 titles. One of the titles was "Chicken Soup for the Spirit," which became the *Chicken Soup for the Soul* book series. It has since sold millions of books and products!

Here are empowering questions:

1. How can I use my talents to make products that will bring terrific value to others and wealth to my family and me?

2. What do I need to learn next so that I make a breakthrough in creating wealth?

3. How may I serve for the good of everyone involved?

Secret 3: Capture Your Ideas

This next step, after asking good questions, demonstrates the difference between wishful thinking and raising your life to higher levels of productivity and enjoyment. You must capture your ideas immediately as they rise to your awareness. Your intuition often gives you gifts. Imagine the times when you had a thought, such as, "If only I had XY, I could fix this situation quickly." A few years later, you saw just such a product on the market. The universe gave many people that idea, but only a few took action. I have a little address book in which I capture my ideas for book titles. Using the address book's alphabetized sections, I can easily access the titles I've noted.

Don't let the thought "I don't know anything about XY" stop you. You can find out. A quick Google search can be your start. Be sure to carry a notebook in your pocket or purse at all times. Some of my clients prefer to carry a digital audio recorder.*

Secret 4: Create a Franchise

Creating a franchise can be a six-step process. Keep reading and I'll show you how.

I have learned the following from C.J. Hayden. Her book, *Get Clients Now*, details a methodology for experiencing ease while effectively gaining clients. To guarantee continued sales of her book, C.J. created the Licensee Kit, a program in which personal

....

* A diminutive MP3 player with voice recording function can be had online for as little as $35. For much less, memory can be added to many cell phones allowing their use as dictation devices. And all PCs can be used likewise, though desktop units may required the addition of a mic.

coaches use her book and methodology for their clients. To use C.J.'s successful program, coaches must ask their clients to buy copies of *Get Clients Now*. As I write this, the *Basic Training, Facilitator's Kit & Renewable Teaching License* is priced at $595.

From C.J.'s example, we learn to move beyond trading time for money. As a personal coach, C.J. can only make an hourly fee. But the magic happened when she made the shift to being the creator of a franchise.

As we see from the C.J. Hayden example, by franchising we are talking about licensing a methodology. We also see that "sudden profits" arise from experience that a work-life has already created. For example, managers can leverage their knowledge by training others. The Internet is a prime place to sell information/training. A seasoned manager can write something about "what to expect in your first year as a manager and how to avoid the big mistakes … by someone who has been there and thrived." So in this case, the "sudden profits" arise from abilities and experiences developed over time. But the new source of income (books and audio programs) brings new profits. Once again, one is reaching beyond an hourly wage. However, be aware the process of creating a franchise may involved CPAs, lawyers, and government agencies, among others.

Six steps to build a franchise

1. Identify a base of skill and knowledge that you are adept with.

2. Design a training seminar to impart that knowledge to audiences.

3. Design teaching aids necessary to put on the seminar (visual aids, lecture notes, discussion questions, model exercises, etc.).

4. Draft a licensing agreement, setting forth responsibilities, nondisclosures, royalties, and warranties.

5. Produce a marketing plan and description of the business model, including projections of potential income with appropriate disclaimers.

6. Market the business model to trainers and, preferably, train them.

The franchise can be a source of sudden profits, because when you use the Internet and good e-newsletter subscriber lists, you can get *a rush of orders.* The holiday season (November and December) can be an amazing time for sales.

Secret 5: Learn an Empowering Definition of Expert

Don't let the thought "I'm not an expert" shut you down. Author Bob Bly* wrote that an expert "had taken what is known in a field and synthesized it into a clear process or system that people like, can understand, and find useful." Above, you see that the six Steps to Build a Franchise is an example of synthesizing

....

* Also known as Robert W. Bly, not to confused with the eminent poet Robert Bly.

ideas into a clear process. You'll also notice that I gave them to you after sharing a real life example.

With my clients, I make the point, "An expert provides a clear system that people like and use."

> *Everyone has been made for some*
> *particular work, and the desire for that*
> *work has been put in every heart.*

RUMI

Bob Bly continues, "I consider myself a scholar or at least a student of my topic, direct mail. I attend workshops and conferences, subscribe to industry periodicals, study the direct mail that crosses my desk each day, read numerous books on direct marketing, and regularly exchange results on what's working with clients, colleagues, and competitors. Therefore, when I offer myself as a leading expert to clients I do it with a clear conscience, knowing I have done everything in my power to make that claim legitimate ... I strive to be the best direct mail copywriter I can be, which is all anyone can ask."

Kristine Carlson, author of *Don't Sweat the Small Stuff for Women* wrote in the beginning section of that book: "I'd like you to know that the advice in this book is not coming from a woman who has any sort of superiority complex or any illusion that she has it all together. Far from it: I'm a normal everyday person who has either dealt with, or is currently dealing with, most of the issues and challenges in this book."

Kristine took herself off the hook by acknowledging that she wasn't perfect in the strategies that followed.

As an author, you don't need to portray yourself as perfect. Instead, *seek to be helpful.*

Secret 6: Get Access to Ideas & Techniques Beyond Yourself

Congratulations to you for reading this book! This simple action makes you extraordinary. How is that possible? The reason is that I have heard many people say "I don't know anything about that," and they drop the subject right there. But you are getting access to new ideas and techniques. Well done!

My client, Marta, has dyslexia – reading is difficult for her. She takes action anyway and listens to audio CDs in her car.

Secret 7: Make Sure You are Coachable

To be coachable is to be humble enough to allow others to teach you new things. The know-it-alls run up against the ceiling of their limited knowledge. Humble people have more opportunities. Author Hal Urban identified these consistent actions of humble people:

1. Humble people treat others with respect.

2. Humble people are thankful.

3. Humble people are genuine.

4. Humble people want to learn and become better.

In my college classes, I talk about *healthy humility*. This includes being coachable.

Secret 8: Listen

Humble people listen. They notice when they have strayed from effective listening, and they bring their attention back to the speaker. Authors Paul J. Donoghue and Mary E. Siegel wrote that the following elements prevent us from listening:

- Defending
- "Me, too" identifying
- Advice giving
- Judging the speaker

Now, I'll give an example of each one:

- **Defending:** "That's not true. I did that in February … February 2nd!"

- **"Me, too" identifying:** "Oh yeah! That happened to me last week. It was awful …"

- **Advice giving:** "You know what I would do about that. First, you need to …"

- **Judging the speaker:** "Come on! Haven't you got over that yet?" (Sometimes, when we hold this idea in our minds, our face and body language show that we have tuned out.)

These errors take the light off the speaker and shine it on the other person. The solution is to observe when these things happen and direct your attention to listening again. You can recover by asking a gentle question. Even a simple one like

"How did it feel when …?" can help. When we listen, we learn new things. While listening, we build strong relationships that can lead to breakthroughs in prosperity.

Secret 9: Align With People Who've Done Part of the Work

When you want sudden profits, you learn to align with people who are already moving forward. For example, I wrote an e-book, *Darkest Secrets of Persuasion Masters: How to Protect Yourself and Turn the Power to Good.* My friend, author David Barron, had an e-newsletter subscriber list of thousands of people. He sent out two e-mail messages to his list, and we both made money when the orders rushed in. Now, that's an example of sudden profits.

David told me about how he put together a program and teamed up with another author. One e-mail campaign gave David a portion of the profits that totaled $6,000. How fun!

Secret 10: Take Action Now! Take a Calculated Risk!

My client, Adriana, wanted to write a book. But she was afraid of having 3,000 copies piled in her garage. I informed her the recent printing innovations known as Print-on-Demand. Using this process, Adriana was able to do a first run of about 30 books for only $150. On her second run, she changed the cover. The point is that Adriana took action. She took a calculated risk.

Remember to make space for your intuition. Inform your intuition and ask your intuition.

Principle:

Intuit to do it!

Power Question:

How can you make space for your intuition?

11

Create (Don't Compete)

How can you avoid a lot of wasted energy and misery?
Avoid unnecessary comparison and competition. To
function on the QuickBreakthrough Level, it is better to focus
on creating, not competing.

Creating is about unleashing your natural brilliance.

I know professional speakers who have a powerful ability to
express compassion, but who discount that ability and focus
on the lack of intense energy that they appear to have when
they compare themselves to Anthony Robbins. This is a waste
of energy and time. It would be better for them to accentuate
their natural brilliance and celebrate how they naturally serve
others well.

You need to be your best self,
not a mediocre copy of someone else.

Let the Competitive Idea Float Away

The idea *Create (don't compete)* is to let a competitive thought float away as if it were a leaf on a river. This is the *Floating Leaves Method.*

For example, a salesperson, Akiko, has the thought, "I don't have the smooth-talking way of our top salesperson, Gary." If Akiko focuses on this thought, it can lead her into a downward spiral. That is, she can unleash a pattern of thoughts that make her feel depressed and even fearful of making her next cold call to a prospective customer.

On the other hand, Akiko can let the disempowering thought float away and replace it with "I have a compassionate way of listening to people and putting them at ease." This is an empowering way for Akiko to be *creative.* She can create and write down compassionate questions to ask her prospective customers so they want to talk with her! She can also remember that many effective salespeople have either an accent or a speech impediment, but they are terrific listeners.

An interviewer responded, "Really? I've always thought good salespeople were smooth talkers."

"For their talking to be effective," I replied, "they need to ask questions and *listen* for what really matters to the buyer. For example, if Sherrie, in her heart of hearts, wants to get a luxury car to prove to herself that she has 'arrived,' then an ineffective car-salesperson could turn her off by talking about gas mileage and space for carpooling children around." Researchers have noted that effective listening helps close sales.*

To switch from a competitive thought to a creative thought, memorize a switch-phrase.

The important process is to switch the direction of your thoughts as fast as possible. Akiko's switch-phrase is "I have a compassionate way of listening." These seven words literally switch the direction of her thoughts, avoiding a downward spiral.

Some people are concerned that their appearance is not stereotypically attractive. They can use the phrase, "I choose what's attractive, not the media."

Let's remember to focus on being creative when we have a competitive thought.

Principle:

When in discomfort, find a way to be creative.

Power Questions:

What bothers you? How can you find a way to become creative? How can you work with your situation in ways that avoid competition?

----

* C. Sorensen, Marketing Manager, OPC-Marketing, wrote about "13 Key Fundamentals to Listening and Closing the Sale," which includes a process to: "think like the customer… limit and control how much talking you do… listen for ideas and concepts, not just words… learn to love pauses… [and] ask questions."

12

Kindle Brand

Part 1

What would you do if you could instantly persuade someone that you are trustworthy? Would you close sales? Would you make your own business a success? Would you perform well in an interview and gain your dream job?

Yes! Your personal brand is the shortest distance to trust. Using a personal brand is using effective communication skills. It is also part of the process of rising to the QuickBreakthrough Level. As I mentioned earlier, on the QuickBreakthrough Level, you have rapport with people and can even get access to *their* intuition!

Look at four examples of personal brands:

- Tom Marcoux, America's Communication Coach
- Jon Gordon, America's #1 Energy Coach
- Marcia Wieder, America's Dream Coach
- The "Go-to" Person for software questions

In my book, *Wake Up Your Spirit to Prosperity,* I discuss the power of a personal brand. Your personal brand can be your key to *sudden profits*, because when people know who you are and what you're offering – and they trust you – your income increases. You make more sales or you earn promotions and raises.

> *The center of personal branding is this question:*
> *What am I best known for?*

When I think, *What am I best known for?* two people I know come to mind. We'll call them George and Sam. Although George and Sam had been good friends for 15 years, they never traveled together. So they decided to take a trip. They said, "To save money, let's share a room with two beds."

Now, George didn't tell Sam about his snoring. I mean the kind of snoring that sounds like a saw: Szing-Ga, Szing-Ga.

On the first night of their trip, at 2:30 a.m., George started to snore. *Bing!* Sam's eyes popped open. He put in earplugs, but the snoring went right through them. Szing-Ga, Szing-Ga.

Sam, a kindly friend, didn't want to wake George up. If he did so, both of them would be hurting the next day. Sam faced a dilemma. To get a second room at 2:30 a.m., he would need to waken George, who had the AAA card needed to get a room at a discount.

Sam had an idea. He needed to put a door between him and George's snoring. So he took the pillows off his bed and put them on the floor of the bathroom. He grabbed the blankets off his bed, too, and locked the bathroom door, because he knew that about three hours later, George would wake up and need to use the restroom. Sam didn't want to get hit in the head by the door!

Sure enough, about four hours later, KNOCK-KNOCK-KNOCK. Sam woke up. He was totally disoriented. "Where am I?" he thought. "I'm on the *floor*! In a bathroom, in a hotel!"

The next day, they got separate rooms, because Sam was not stupid!

What do you think Sam is best known for? Being respectful. And coming up with a creative solution in a tough situation. What is George best known for?

Snoring!

I'm sharing this story for two reasons. It's entertaining and it points to how a good story can emphasize a personal characteristic that distinguishes a person in the marketplace. *Sam is good at coming up with a creative solution in a tough situation.*

Sharing a story that illustrates a desired characteristic is a vital part of your personal brand.

Here are the elements of your personal brand:

- The answer to "What am I best known for?"
- A story that moves emotions
- A memorable phrase
- A label
- A sound bite

Here's how Sam's story might fill in his personal brand elements:

The answer to "What am I best known for?"

Being respectful and creative.

A story that moves emotions

Sam protects his friend's rest by sleeping on the bathroom floor of his hotel room.

A memorable phrase

When the going gets tough, Sam gets creative.

A label

Sam is a creative solution-finder.

A sound bite

When the going gets tough, Sam gets creative (in this case, it's same as our memorable phrase).

Now it's your turn. Please fill in the form on the next page:

Your Personal Brand Worksheet

Fill in the blanks

1. What am I best known for?

2. A story that moves emotions

3. A memorable phrase

4. A label

5. A sound bite

Remember that using your personal brand is part of rising to the QuickBreakthrough Level. As I mentioned, your hidden power is the ability to shift to the QuickBreakthrough Level. Using the powerful communication skills of the personal brand, you are able to connect with people on a heart-to-heart level.

Principle:

Your personal brand is the shortest distance to trust.

Power Question:

What is your answer to "What are you best known for?"

Part 2 of Kindle Brand

In the previous section, I mentioned that your personal brand is the shortest distance to trust. The personal brand tells people: "You can trust that this is who I am and this is what I will do."

Similarly, a brand on the company level is about the team: "This is who *we* are and what we will do." It is about identity and action. To create and maintain an effective company brand, we need to hone our communication skills.

With terrific communication skills, we easily rise to the QuickBreakthrough Level. Salespeople who create a rapport with prospective customers gain more sales. Managers who use the methods I reveal in this section create *synergy* – a situation in which the thoughts and energy of five people equal the power of ten or more. Effective teams come up with ideas and methods that *open the door to sudden profits.*

Years ago, when I worked for a particular corporation, I was stunned by how wasteful and ineffective the meetings were. With ten people in a room and three hours invested, thousands of dollars were wasted. I vowed to learn how to lead effective meetings.

Now, we will talk about skills for *Streamlined Power Meetings*. We use the P.O.W.E.R.—M.E.E.T. Process:

> P – Prepare
>
> O – Own ideas
>
> W – Write
>
> E – Engage listening
>
> R – Recognize everyone
>
> M – Mention targets
>
> E – Encourage criteria
>
> E – Enrich efforts
>
> T – Track

Note: Many of these communication skills are also helpful for personal relationships.

The ability to effectively lead Streamlined Power Meetings gives you a true advantage. You can create abundant good will that can lead to breakthroughs!

Prepare

What's the fastest way to keep a meeting on track and make it brief? Prepare and write an agenda. Even before an impromptu

P
O
W
E
R
•
M
E
E
T

meeting, write five points to be covered. (Even a handwritten list works). Make photocopies and distribute them.

Sometimes, it is better to start a presentation by asking "What were you hoping or expecting we would talk about?" On a flip chart, write down the attendees' answers. This will give attendees a positive emotional connection.

Preparation is powerful, even when you're not the team leader. You are *still* the leader of your own idea or your own campaign, and you want to appear as competent and effective as you truly are. The important principle is "Courage is easier when I'm prepared."

Principle:

Courage is easier when I'm prepared.

Power Questions:

How can you prepare for an upcoming meeting or event? Who can help you double-check your work?

Own Ideas

Have you noticed how many of us have been conditioned from childhood to compete? A helpful plan is to *own ideas as a group*. During meetings, we need to avoid situations that become a contest of egos.

In an earlier chapter, I emphasized the power of *Create (don't compete)*. At a meeting, it is best when the whole group owns the ideas. Write each idea down on a flip chart with no reference to the person who voiced it. This avoids a contest to see which team member's idea wins. Ideas are written as neutral elements that the team is considering.

Author Jason Jennings wrote: "[To truly motivate workers, have] an authentic cause that becomes the culture of the company." For example, for Pepsi, it came down to two words: "Beat Coke." The effective leader helps the team *voice an authentic cause and own the ideas* to make the team successful.

The Smart Step

The age old team building adage says, "There is no 'I' in 'team.'" This *sounds* nice. But we know that 'I' is predominant in the thoughts and feelings of many of us.

The Smart Step is to help *yourself* attach both team benefits and personal benefits to necessary actions. It follows this format:

When the team gains _____, I gain _____.

Some examples

- When the team gains the Kervin Account, I build up good will that I can use to get time for my family's vacation.

- When I guide the team to feel good about working together, *I feel good* about coming to work.

People take action for multiple reasons. You unleash positive power when you make the multiple benefits clear and connect them to people's emotions.

Principle:

Own ideas as a group.

Power Question:

How can you use a good structure to decrease the emergence of individual egos during the meeting?

Write

P
O
w
E
R
·
M
E
E
T

Did you ever endure a meeting and, at the end, wonder, "What did we accomplish?" The way to have the answer at your fingertips is to designate one person as the Recorder. This person writes down people's comments on large sheets of paper ("the group memory") taped to a wall. These pages can be rolled up after the meeting and given to an administrative staff person to type. Also, designate one person as the Facilitator to run the meeting. She makes sure everyone contributes. Often, it is better when the supervisor avoids acting as the Facilitator, because many team members will censor themselves when they watch the supervisor's reactions.

You want a free flow of ideas during the brainstorming part of your meeting.

A Recorder and a Facilitator help you squeeze more value out of your group's meeting. As I mentioned earlier, many years ago at a particular major corporation, I was stunned by how poorly the meetings were run. With ten people in the room during a 3-hour meeting, thousands of dollars were wasted. I learned that having a Recorder and Facilitator were prime ways to squeeze more value out of a meeting.

Now, in my company, we conduct meetings in which powerful leaps forward are accomplished. What a relief!

Principle:

Engage a Recorder and a Facilitator to squeeze more value out of your group's meeting.

Power Questions:

How can you make being a Recorder or a Facilitator into positions that are attractive to team members? Can you rotate the positions?

Engage Listening

Imagine the times you have heard a wife, husband, or teenager say that someone "is not listening to me!" Listening helps us create rapport. The *Merriam-Webster's Online Dictionary* defines *rapport* as:

> *Relation characterized by harmony,*
> *conformity, accord, or affinity.*

As team leaders and team members, we realize that nothing gets done without rapport. People need to align with each other in a spirit of connection and cooperation to make big things happen.

P
O
W
E
R
•
M
E
E
T

> *Many hands, hearts, and minds generally*
> *contribute to anyone's notable achievement.*

WALT DISNEY

The idea is to create rapport. Then the team pulls together in one direction.

> *When you're listening, you're creating rapport.*

Often, meetings involve emotionally charged topics. In such situations, listening to the other person first works well.

To deepen the listening and help the other person feel, "I'm being heard," we learn to express *Listening Questions*.

Listening Questions help us demonstrate our attention to and concern for the person who is talking.

Listening Questions

1. That sounds like it was frustrating for you. What happened next?

2. What's most important to you about this situation?

3. Would you prefer that I only listen, or would you like me to brainstorm with you?

Gently Express What You Heard & Ask for Confirmation

It helps to say, "I want to be sure I understand what you're talking about. Let me tell you what I heard. If I didn't get it right, you can give me more details." Then repeat what you heard using many of the exact words. Avoid paraphrasing, because you could stray from what the person meant.

Like any technique, the *Express What You Heard and Ask for Confirmation* technique can fail to work with certain individuals. Then, we become more subtle. We reply with comments like: "So it's most important to you that we do _____?"

Finally, listening involves being silent, good eye contact, and leaning forward slightly (to convey interest).

Principle:

When you're listening, you're building rapport.

Power Questions:

How can you increase your ability to use Listening Questions? Can you practice in the car on your way to work?

Recognize Everyone

Recognize everyone's contribution. The Facilitator encourages participation. She makes an appreciative comment like: "Thanks Bob, for putting that idea into the soup."

> *The deepest principle in human nature is the craving to be appreciated.*
>
> WILLIAM JAMES

P
O
W
E
R
•
M
E
E
T

When I meet someone, I imagine her wearing an invisible sign that says, 'Make me feel important!' ... This is one of the most important lessons in dealing with people I have ever learned.

MARY KAY ASH
founder of Mary Kay Cosmetics

It helps to write up a list of appreciative comments and practice them on your own. An appreciative comment does *not* work if it is used repeatedly during a meeting.

Here are some examples:

1. Thanks for that idea, Mary. This leads us into the next phase of Project XY.

2. Thank you, Julio. I was hoping someone would raise that topic. Now, we'll be able to handle customer concerns about ____.

3. Good point, Sarah. That reminds us to focus on ____.

Principle:

Express appreciation for each person's contribution, and you open the door to good feelings.

Power Question:

How can you express appreciation in various ways?

Mention Targets

Mention targets, both in numbers and a vision. As I wrote earlier, Pepsi had a goal or vision, "Beat Coke!" Team goals must be in writing and must be *measurable*. The vision must be backed up with numbers. How many sales must be accomplished this week, this month and this year to achieve your vision? Put up a scoreboard so everyone can see it.

Author Zig Ziglar talked about how people would *not* go bowling if they could not see the bowling pins drop. Your scoreboard helps team members see the bowling pins drop. Effective team leaders know how to show the group that progress is being made.

Principle:

Targets expressed in both numbers and a vision are motivating and attainable.

Power Question:

How can you use some form of a scoreboard so the team can "see the bowling pins drop"?

Encourage

How can people feel true encouragement? They feel great when they see progress being made.

The first step is to *Set Criteria for Excellence*. When a complicated solution is needed, encourage the group to note aspects of an ideal solution. You *set criteria* for what a good solution would look like.

Be Sure to Set Criteria for Excellence

The idea is to identify what creates excellent results. Often, we need to avoid getting bogged down in trying to make things perfect. Instead, we can focus on a project that creates *excellent* results.

For example, years ago, I considered making a short film entitled *Dimension Man*. First, I set criteria for a project that was both feasible and worthwhile:

1. A film that was edgy

2. A film that was simple enough to produce quickly (because I was pre-booked with other projects)

3. A film that had both a startling first image and final image

4. A film that had characteristics that would make it a likely contest winner

5. A film with a modest budget

With the criteria set up, I could, as the leader, evaluate whether the project was a "go" or if it would be better to abandon it.

To create consensus, sometimes it's easier to have people toss in ideas about what a good solution will look like. Then, the Facilitator can say, "Well, it looks like this solution matches criteria 1, 2, and 3. How about if we move forward with this solution?"

Principle:

Encourage your team to *Set Criteria for Excellence* to improve results.

Power Question:

How can you help the team *Set Criteria for Excellence*?

Enrich Efforts

Sometimes, as a team member, you witness a motion pass or resolution being accepted that you feel is inappropriate. When that happens, it is often effective to say something like: "As you know, I was initially not for Project A. But now that it has been accepted, I will devote my full support to it." This is the process of sowing seeds of good will. Sometime in the future, you may call on others for their support when you are pressing to pass a resolution of your own.

You're letting the team know that you will *enrich the team efforts*. You are demonstrating that you are a team player. When you first examined "Project A," you may have had limited perceptions. By saying that you will devote your full support, you give yourself a graceful way to back down from your original position.

The battlefield refrain goes, "Don't focus *only* on winning the battle – you might lose the war." Similarly, at work, the higher priority is to be seen as a devoted, loyal, and competent team member.

Principle:

Expressing unity with team goals builds your position and gives your future resolutions a better chance of being accepted.

Power Question:

How can you demonstrate that you are on the same page as the team in terms of goals and effort?

Track

As we discussed earlier in this section, the large sheets of paper tacked to the wall by the Recorder form the *group memory*. Near the end of the meeting, it is crucial to note tasks, people's names, and due dates. This is part of the process of *tracking* tasks and results. The Facilitator makes sure that group members take the time to make reasonable and actual commitments to tasks and due dates. He or she invites people to open their day planners and note the due dates.

I advise my clients to note three important things:

1. Effort Goals

2. Result Goals

3. The Group Scoreboard

Here are examples:

1. An Effort Goal: Each team member agrees to make 15 sales prospecting calls a day.

2. A Result Goal: The team closes five extra sales in the first week.

3. The leader posts a whiteboard in the main room. On the whiteboard, the team leader notes these factors: (1) a line-graph showing how many calls each person makes each day and (2) the score, which is the number of closed sales that have occurred in the week so far.

Using a team scoreboard helps develop cooperation among team members. One manager was amazed when his team members, *on their own*, discovered ways to cover the extended work-shifts. The team members were motivated to find solutions because *all team members* were earning an extra $9 per new client engaged.

Researchers have noted that people tend to enjoy playing a game.* I emphasize *Make It a Game You Can Win*. My clients have told me that they have gained good results with the process *Keep Score and Achieve More*.

• •

* "For children, the interesting sounds and colorful graphics make computer games perfect teachers. They 'possess infinite patience and increasingly, can be modified to match the learner's interest,' says Kimberly Burge, senior lecturer in UCI's Department of Education... UCI professor Bonnie Nardi is interested in theory in human-computer interaction and computer-supported collaborative work. She studies *World of Warcraft*, a massive multiplayer online game with more than 8.5 million subscribers. Players create online personas that explore, develop skills, make money and socialize, advancing through 70 levels by mastering certain tasks called quests." From "Calit2 Looks into the Games People Play," Anna Lynn Spitzer (California Institute for TeleCommunications and Information Technology).

How to Lead and Avoid Hovering

Some employees complain about a boss who hovers or breathes down their necks. The solution is to set natural check-in points. The effective team leader can even ask, "When do you think it will be a natural time for us to check in with each other?" The team leader and team members place the natural check-in points on their calendars. In this way, the leader effectively monitors the team members' progress. It is useful to remember that "You get what you inspect" and "What gets rewarded, gets repeated."

Encourage tracking and group participation.

Remember: Learning the skills to effectively communicate and lead in a group setting helps you rise to the QuickBreakthrough Level. When team members trust you and feel comfortable around you, breakthroughs can appear!

Principle:

Keep score and achieve more.

Power Questions:

How can you measure progress simultaneously in these two areas: Effort Goals and Result Goals? How can you use a Group Scoreboard?

Conclusion of Part II

Imagine that you could instantly become more insightful and powerful. You now have powerful tools embodied in the Q.U.I.C.K. Process:

> Q – Qualify
>
> U – Use Time-Leverage
>
> I – Intuit to Do It!
>
> C – Create (don't compete)
>
> K – Kindle Brand

Remember that your hidden power *is the ability to shift to the QuickBreakthrough Level.* The Q.U.I.C.K. methods are your key to open the door, releasing a huge flow of ideas and actions that create success and fulfillment.

Recalling one idea can send you soaring forward. You have the power to choose your beliefs and how you live on a daily basis. You can choose to focus on scarcity or abundance. By choosing abundance, I mean choosing the perspective of seeing the glass as half full. *You can remind yourself to pick abundance with "I am grateful for …"*

Before I go to sleep each night, I write in my Daily Journal of Victories and Blessings. A victory relates to an action I took, such as exercising. A blessing is a gift, such as talking on the telephone with an extended family member, My perspective is to approach the small, positives things in life as gifts, to be appreciated, rather than expected. I go to sleep feeling grateful for the adventures and blessings I enjoy each day.

I am grateful for the opportunity to connect with you through this book. I wish you a journey of love, abundance, and blessings. Let's continue with the next section.

Part III

13

10 Best Kept Secrets of Persuasion Masters

Introduction

In Part I, you learned the B.E.S.T. Principles so *nothing can stop you.*

In Part II, you learned how to rise to the QuickBreakthrough Level. I emphasized, *your hidden power is the ability to shift to the QuickBreakthrough Level.* On this Level, your intuition helps you make leaps forward for your success and fulfillment.

Now, in Part III, you will learn the *10 Best Kept Secrets of Persuasion Masters.* Persuasion Masters function on the QuickBreakthrough Level. They are masters in creating rapport with other people. Through rapport and effective persuasion, Persuasion Masters gain cooperation and sales. They even gain access to other people's intuition!

This section will guide you in various methods that will enable you to become an Effective Persuader. The Effective Persuader saves time and gets more done. The Effective Persuader also eliminates time wasted due to misunderstandings. And let's face it, the Effective Persuader *gets what he or she wants* through the cooperation of other people.

Also, as I mentioned in Part I, Chapter 1, learning the skills of Persuasion Masters provides an *Easethrough*™. The Easethrough is better than a standard breakthrough, because it removes resistance. Persuasion Masters demonstrate skills to *remove the resistance in a listener or customer.*

Often the best way to learn something is to see the process. So I will show how I start many of my speeches about powerful persuasion. First, I hand out a worksheet. Then I begin:

> My name is Tom Marcoux. I'm known as "America's Communication Coach." The *San Francisco Examiner* has also called me the "Personal Branding Instructor."
>
> What counts today is that we get you the most benefit from our time together. Now, I have a question for you: *What did you hope or expect that I'd talk about?* I'll write your comments down here.
>
> [The audience responds, and I write their comments on a flip chart.]
>
> I have just demonstrated two of the ten principles, or powerful secrets, of persuasion. These secrets will empower your presentations.
>
> On your work sheet, please fill in the blank space next to Secret 6 with these words: "A is for 'Ask questions.'"
>
> Beside Secret 8, please write: "I is for 'Increase Listening.'"

I have shared this opening section of my speech to show you persuasion in action. One of my top goals is to establish a rapport with my audience. To do that, I ask questions and listen to their answers.

Persuasion is Helping

Now, let's be absolutely clear, *persuasion* is defined as "communication intended to induce belief or action."

But let's make the following empowering distinction for our purposes:*

- Persuasion is helpful because we start with the benefits for your listener in mind.

- Manipulation is a dark practice when someone selfishly focuses solely on his or her own benefit to the exclusion of concerns for the listener's welfare.

Fortunately, our focus is on rising to the positive Quick-Breakthrough Level *so we concentrate on positive persuasion.* We will use the 10-point P.E.R.S.U.A.S.I.O.N. Process.

P – Prepare

E – Emotionalize

R – Reveal Benefits

S – Set Up Similarities and Participation

U – Unleash Stories

••••••••••••••••••••••••••••••••••

* I acknowledge that this is a sharper distinction than is routinely recognized, as reflected in the quoted definition, but it will serve us well.

A – Ask Questions

S – Show Your Personal Brand

I – Increase Listening

O – Organize Personaltainment Branding™

N – Nurture Trust

In this section, I will use the label *Buyer* to represent anyone you wish to persuade. You want the person to *buy into* the ideas, product, or service that you're presenting.

Read on, and you're on your way to being an Effective Persuader and to gaining what you want in life.

14

Prepare

Courage is easier when you're prepared. When you are serious about persuasion, you will do what it takes to be well-prepared.

An interviewer asked me, "To become prepared, are you trying to figure out what the Buyer wants or needs? How do you know what's good for that person?"

I replied, "Two elements of preparation will enable you to present a buffet table of benefits so the Buyer can identify what's most important to him or her."

The first element is to get to know your product so well that you know the value it provides. Talk with previous buyers and get testimonials.

The second element is to think deeply about the Buyer's situation.

Persuasion Master: Fred Bettger

Here is an example of thinking deeply about the Buyer's situation. Fred Bettger, author of *How I Raised Myself from*

Failure to Success in Selling, describes how he sold a businessman life insurance and protected the man's business at the same time. Mr. Booth, was shopping for life insurance so he could borrow $250,000 to save his business. The creditors insisted that Mr. Booth have life insurance to cover that $250,000. Fred Bettger paused, did his preparation, and realized what Mr. Booth's *most vulnerable point* was. The businessman's vulnerable point was that he could lose the loan if he kept on procrastinating. He needed to take his medical exam as soon as possible or something might show up on the exam that would result in the cancellation of both the insurance and the $250,000 line of credit. Then his business would be in trouble.

When Fred Bettger identified Mr. Booth's most vulnerable point, he made an appointment for him to have a medical exam with a top medical examiner on the same day that he and Mr. Booth were scheduled to meet. At the meeting, he explained to Mr. Booth what would be at stake if he delayed choosing an insurance provider.

This example shows the power of effective preparation for successful persuasion. Fred Bettger was selling life insurance – but he also helped Mr. Booth get his $250,000 loan and save his business.

Fred Bettger focused on two important questions in his preparation:

> *Exercise:* Think of your potential customer (or perhaps, a family member you want to persuade). Identify the following:

1. What is the key issue for that person?

2. What is the most vulnerable point?

Preparation Includes Knowing Personal Details

In my audio program with workbook, *How Top Salespeople Double Sales in Half the Time,* I emphasize the use of the "How I Can Help Plan." This is a worksheet that you fill out for each important prospective customer. Write down details about:

1. The person's hobbies

2. Family members' hobbies

3. College attended

4. Birthday

5. Possible ways for the person to benefit in her business

6. Any other details

Before you meet with the person, review these details. Then you can find ways to help the person, and you demonstrate that you care.

Preparation Includes Rehearsing

When I say rehearsing, I mean memorizing certain word patterns that will enable you to speak clearly and concisely and engage your listener's emotions.

To engage a person's emotions, use a *word picture*. This is the technique of using words to create an emotional picture in the Buyer's mind. Here's a word picture that I have used:

> *"When I'm waiting for you, I feel like a puppy adrift*
> *on a raft in the middle of the Atlantic Ocean – lost and*
> *not knowing if the rescue boat will ever arrive."*

I used this word picture to communicate with a former girlfriend. One member of the audience asked, "Did it work?" I replied: "Yes. If it hadn't, I wouldn't be telling you about it."

rendered by Chris Sehenuk

In business, a word picture could like this:

> *"Our approach is to safeguard your data like a bulldog*
> *with his bone – in Fort Knox!"*

Preparation Helps You Identify a Person's "Hot Button"

A "hot button"* is something that's tied into a person's deepest desires and, sometimes, concerns.

For example, one of Walt Disney's team members said, "If you ever wanted a conversation with Mr. Disney, all you had to do was ask, "How's the [Disneyland] park going, [Walt]?" That was the magic question! Walt would drop what he was doing, take the inquirer to see scale models and show him or her the latest innovation for Disneyland. Walt loved to talk about Disneyland.

This is the power of preparation. When you find out what really excites a person (his or her "hot button"), you make a friend. And persuasion becomes much easier.

Persuasion Master: Harvey MacKay

An important part of preparation is focusing on what a person really wants. Here is how Harvey MacKay, author of *Swim with the Sharks without Getting Eaten Alive*, connected so well with CNN television host Larry King that he has been on the show six times!

Harvey knew that Larry King had written books. And he had *special information* to help Larry sell more books. When the men happened to share a limousine ride, Harvey offered Larry the following details to help him sell more books.

••••••••••••••••••••••••••••••••••

* In the field of sales, a hot button is a trigger to someone making a buying decision, as noted by author Brian Tracy. On the other hand, in daily life, it refers to an area of sensitivity in a person that may lead to intense emotion.

Ingram Book Group* is the second largest U.S. wholesaler of books. If Larry would go to Nashville and give a short speech to the 100-person sales force, the salespeople would talk up his book and place more copies in bookstores.

Then Harvey talked about his meeting with the president of Barnes & Noble/B. Dalton. Harvey explained that he had told the president that he was going on a 35-city tour and that he would talk up the B&N stores on every radio and TV show he was on. He convinced the president to raise the B. Dalton order from 1,500 to 15,000 copies of his book. Harvey then went to Waldenbooks and asked why they planned to order just a token number of books when B. Dalton had ordered 15,000. Seven days later Waldenbooks raised their order to 15,000.

The point is that Harvey gave Larry King *news he could use.*

Harvey says, "In networking, you're only as good as what you give away."

How did Harvey get his special knowledge? Through preparation. He gave himself a six-month self-taught course on the publishing business. This included talking with 30 authors, many literary agents, 12 publishers, several promotional firms, and six lawyers.

Often, we can begin our preparation with the use of search engines like Google.com. It feels great to get started.

....

* Since the turn of the millenium, Ingram BG has experienced steady double digit sales contraction due to a collapse of traditional patterns in book sales.

Principle:

Courage is easier when I'm prepared. Good preparation leads to great persuasion.

Power Questions:

How can you prepare? What keywords do you want to put into a search engine like Google.com? Which people can answer your questions? What is the most vulnerable point for your prospective customer?

15

Emotionalize

The right margin has vertical letters spelling PERSUASION.

A l Gilbert, known as the eight-million dollar man (the level of deals he closes), told me, "People buy on emotion and later justify on facts."*

When I say *emotionalize*, I am talking about utilizing this *buy on emotion* insight. To emotionalize is to use words that connect with the Buyer's emotions.

Secret Persuasion Skill: Connect With a Person's Desired Identity

Identity is the sense: *This is who I am.* We see the idea of identity in the book, *The Power of Cult Branding* by Matthew W. Ragas and B. J. Bueno.

A reader at Amazon.com described the details of this book:

• •

* It is unclear who first said this, but it is an oft repeated adage of sales.

All of the brands featured in the book facilitate people getting together so they can go and be with their 'own kind.' At these events, customers of these brands can form extended families that share the same value system that they do. It's a practical guide to how a company can help and reward their loyal customers by supporting them, helping the customers to achieve fulfillment in their lives. Take [Harley-Davidson], for example. They host bike week events and support bike clubs; Vans Shoes builds skate parks; Jimmy Buffet does music that strikes a chord with people of many different backgrounds. They form groups that support and help each other.

Persuasion Master: Oprah Winfrey

Oprah Winfrey said: "Though I'm grateful for the blessings of wealth, it hasn't changed who I am. My feet are still on the ground. I'm just wearing better shoes."

This comment makes me think of Oprah's appeal. People can relate to her as a regular person who also has a current life of abundance and wealth. Oprah's audience knows that she began in poverty and was abused as a child. They know that Oprah, like millions of Americans, has had a yo-yo battle with weight for many years. When Oprah interviews someone, her emotions and genuine concern are visible on her face. Oprah is *real* to her viewers. And it doesn't hurt when viewers see how generous she is with her gifts to her in-studio audience. The gifts of new cars brought her in-studio audience to a near frenzy of joy and excitement.

Sometimes, Oprah's broadcast audience is estimated at over 70 million viewers. Each viewer takes on a form of the identity that is summed up in Oprah's catchphrase from her Web site: "Live Your Best Life." This clear idea carries through Oprah's television show, her book, *Live Your Best Life*, and her magazine, *O*.

Principle:

Persuade through emotions that are connected to identity.

Power Questions:

What details are part of the identity that a particular person wants to have? How can you make your product or service connect with that person's identity?

16

Reveal Benefits

How do you seize a person's attention? How can you share the benefits of your idea, product, or service in compelling ways? If the problem is that you don't yet know enough about what is important to the person, you ask effective questions. Based on the person's answers, you learn the best order in which to reveal the benefits of your product or service.

Researchers note that people stay on automatic pilot while they are on a constant vigil for "what's in it for me?"* Everyone is looking for the answers to: "How can I avoid pain and things that make me fearful?" and "How can I get what I want?"

● ●

* Wayne Froggatt, Consultant Director of the Centre for Rational Emotive Behaviour Therapy, London, and Director of the New Zealand Centre for Rational Emotive Behaviour Therapy, wrote, "Notwithstanding any precepts which say we 'should' be otherwise, human beings appear to be intrinsically concerned first with their own welfare. Hans Selye has argued that the desire to maintain oneself and stay happy is the most ancient – and one of the most important – impulses that motivates living beings."

As mentioned earlier, people will do more to avoid pain than to gain joy.

A Major Benefit: Prevention of a Loss

The classic book on persuasion is *Influence* by Robert Cialdini. Cialdini emphasizes the power of *scarcity* in terms of persuasion. For example, years ago, I was in an outlet store of a major bookstore chain. I saw only one copy of a particular book. I wasn't sure whether I wanted to buy that book right then – but there was only one copy left! I perceived an apparent scarcity. So, you guessed it: I bought the book immediately.

Car salespeople use scarcity as a tool of persuasion. They say, "I just talked with my manager. I can get you a special discount, but it's only available today. I trust that you don't want to miss this chance."

Persuasion Master: Martin Luther King, Jr.

Martin Luther King, Jr. has been recognized as one of greatest speakers in history. He used vivid word pictures to inspire emotion in his audiences. He revealed *heart-lifting benefits* in his speeches.

For example, at the end of his "I Have a Dream" speech, he seized our emotions when he said:

> "... *when we let freedom ring, when we let it ring from every tenement and every hamlet, from every state and every city, we will be able to speed up that day when all of God's children, black men and white men, Jews and Gentiles, Protestants and Catholics, will be*

> *able to join hands and sing in the words of the old*
> *negro spiritual, 'Free at last, free at last. Thank God*
> *Almighty, we are free at last.'"*

There we have it! One of the greatest benefits that humankind has always longed for: to be free at last!

In a later section entitled *Ask Questions*, I will talk more about the process of effectively asking questions. My point here is that you, as an Effective Persuader, need to complete your preparation by writing a list of powerful benefits of your idea, product, or service. Then, during a conversation with a Buyer, you can ask questions and discover which benefits are most important to him or her.

Learn What Order a Client Wants to Hear Benefits

Mark this powerful question: "What's most important to you about _____?" This will help you discover the person's priorities, emotions, and values.

Sometimes, a prospective customer replies, "What's most important to me is that the product is easy to use, goes with my living room décor, and has a money back guarantee." It is likely that she expressed the first thing that came to mind first and that detail is the most important thing to her. So talk first about how easy the product is to use.

On the other hand, we have a different situation if the customer replies, "Three things are most important to me: price, color, and reliability." Researchers note that "reliability" is likely to be most important to that Buyer.* The reason is that when the Buyer said "three things," he or she invited you to wait for the third item. Talk about reliability first, since you have learned that it is most important to this particular Buyer.

Principle:

Reveal benefits in the order that the client wants to hear about them.

Power Question:

Write down a list of ten benefits of your idea, product, or service for the Buyer. What words about these benefits would stir the person's emotions in your favor?

---

* Authors Gene Bedell and Marshall Sylver discuss how to recognize prospects' true priorities.

17

Set Up Similarities and Participation

People tend to like others who are (or seem) similar to them. The important similarities are traits, concerns, and feelings that they have in common. The Effective Persuader expresses in a manner such as, "Like you, I was initially concerned about _____. Then I learned _____, and I started to feel better about the situation."

Persuasion Master: Anthony Robbins

In a number of workshops, Anthony "Tony" Robbins has the attendees clap their hands in rapid succession while exclaiming *"Yes! Yes! Yes! Whoooah! YES!"* In this manner, he has hundreds of people change their physical state, and all feel a common excitement. Tony stated that he wanted workshop attendees to experience the energized feeling common to sports fans at a game featuring their favorite team. The *"Yes! Whoooah!*

YES!" process is a prime example of Set Up Similarities and Participation.

Just imagine the delighted smiles that the workshop attendees *share* with each other.

In daily life, we can ask gentle questions and help a person access her positive memories and feelings. You can ask, "So what are you looking forward to?" And later, you can ask something like, "Oh, and what feels good about that?" The next step, if possible, is to express how you have experienced something similar. Then, on common ground, you and the person can share a delighted smile.

Help a Person Feel Connected to You

David Barron, persuasion expert and coauthor of *Power Persuasion*, emphasizes that it helps to say "I agree." Saying "I agree" puts the other person at ease.

Persuasion Master: Mahatma Gandhi

A mother brought her son a distance of many miles to ask Gandhi to tell him to stop eating sugar. Gandhi gently replied, "Come back in one week." The mother listened and returned with her son one week later. Gandhi turned to the boy and said, "Stop eating sugar." Distraught, the mother said, "Why didn't you tell him that last week?" Gandhi replied, "Last week, *I* was eating sugar."

We need to be consistent. We need to be genuine. Then we will be Effective Persuaders.

Have the Person Participate in Your Demonstration

The next technique comes from Joel Bauer, coauthor of *How to Persuade People Who Don't Want to Be Persuaded: Get What You Want Every Time!* Joel was talking to a prospective client in her office. She was a manager, and she didn't see any value in Joel being the spokesperson at her tradeshow booth. He had to break her thinking pattern. When he noticed a rubber band encircling her wrist, he asked her to place it across her upper lip. The rubber band was cool to the touch. He asked her to stretch the rubber band and place it back on her lip. Now, the rubber band was warm to the touch. Joel explained that in the same way, he heats up an audience at a tradeshow. Her prospective customers would tune in to his presentation.

"My crowds will pull in more early-adopters than you've ever had, precisely because my crowds are so big, so excited, so full of energy. A crowd draws a larger crowd!," Joel explained to the manager. Joel had successfully seized the manager's attention and gained the contract.

Joel Bauer calls the rubber band technique a Transformation Mechanism, which, he says, is "a trick with a point."

Remember to have your prospective customer participate in your demonstration. For example, my client, Nina provides a calculator so that a prospective customer can type in numbers and prove to herself that she will gain significant savings. Top salespeople emphasize, "People believe what they say [and do] more than what you say."

Principle:

Seize a person's attention by having him or her participate in the demonstration.

Power Questions:

How can you convey that you have traits, concerns and feelings in common with a person? How can you help the person participate in your demonstration?

18

Unleash Stories

When you hear "unleash," what comes to mind? Perhaps unleashing a dog? I say unleash because a story is like a wild animal that has power. A tiger can get us to run. A baby deer can inspire us to say, "Awww, isn't she adorable?"

> *Stories help you connect instantly with the listener. The moment you connect, you both rise to the QuickBreakthrough Level.*

Your hidden power contains the seeds that can make you a good storyteller.

A story can be as brief as one sentence. For example, one of my clients gave me this testimonial: "Using just one of Tom's methods, I got more done in 2 weeks than in 6 months." She was referencing one of the methods in my audio program, *Power Time Management: More Time, Less Stress and Zero Procrastination.*

In my speeches, I sometimes describe this scenario:

> *"When I was hanging onto the hood of a speeding truck by my fingertips, I wasn't thinking about the cameraman who was filming the stunt. I was more concerned about ..."*

About what? This has the element of a good story. The listener needs to respond, "And then what happened?"

Persuasion Master: Jesus of Nazareth

The message of this powerful Persuasion Master has endured for over 2,000 years. Jesus of Nazareth spoke in parables – short stories that illustrate a moral precept.* Jesus' parables often included compelling imagery. Notice the images in the *Parable of the Sower*** from *Matthew 13:3-8 NIV:******

> *A farmer went out to sow his seed. As he was scattering the seed, some fell along the path, and the birds came and ate it up. Some fell on rocky places, where it did not have much soil. It sprang up quickly, because the soil was shallow. But when the sun came up, the plants were scorched, and they withered because they had no root. Other seed fell among thorns, which grew up and choked the plants. Still other seed fell on good soil, where it produced a crop – a hundred, sixty, or thirty times what was sown.*

JESUS OF NAZARETH

....

* Merriam-Webster Online Dictionary. www.merriam-webster.com.

** Sometimes referred to as *The Parable of the Mustard Seed.*

*** *New International Version* of the Bible.

Collect stories in which your product or service saved the day. Rehearse telling the stories with good story elements, such as tension, suspense, and release.

Principle:

Use stories to inspire emotions in the listener; that is, emotions that are favorable to you.

Power Questions:

What stories that reflect the value of what you offer will engage the emotions of the Buyer? Which loved ones will kindly listen to you rehearse your stories?

19

Ask Questions

If I could give you what you really want, would you be interested?

Did I capture your attention?

Asking questions is a powerful way to seize the Buyer's attention and discover how you can best serve his or her needs, desires and well-being.

When I teach persuasion methods in a public speaking course for my graduate students, I emphasize: "I can't persuade you, if I don't know you." Learn to ask effective questions.

Persuasion Master: President John F. Kennedy

President John F. Kennedy said, "Ask not what your country can do for you; ask what you can do for your country." He caught our attention with a powerful question. Answers come up, such as vote and donate time and money to worthy causes.

In other speeches, President John F. Kennedy helped answer his own question by giving us inspiration:

- "I believe that this nation should commit itself to achieving the goal, before this decade is out, of landing a man on the moon and returning him safely to the Earth."

- "Our fears must never hold us back from pursuing our hopes."

President Kennedy helped the United States develop and accept *in the heart* a vision of landing a man on the moon. Similarly, the Effective Persuader asks questions that help Buyers form their own vision of a better life that includes the product or service she or he is marketing.

The important point is to ask questions that help you uncover what is most important to the Buyer. Remember this powerful question: "What is most important to you about ___?"

These are two other good questions:

1. What stands between you and how you would ideally like this situation to be?

2. In order for you to have _____, what has to happen?

Questions are Powerful – But be Careful of the Word "Why"

Asking "Why?" often puts the Buyer on the defensive. The Buyer jumps into his or her head and makes things up that sound like rational reasons. But we want to get to the emotions.

As I mentioned before, people buy based on their emotions and justify their purchase later with facts.

Our solution is to use the word "how" instead of "why." Say something like: "So how does that work for you?" Another powerful word is "what." You could ask, "What would you lose if you didn't get this product today?"

There is one exception to the practice of avoiding the word "why." On a number of occasions, I have asked, "Why don't you take it?" The Buyer thinks for a moment … and then buys my product. Most of the time, it works like a charm.

Another Powerful Word is "Wonder"

You could say, "I wonder how we can take care of the details and make sure you don't miss this opportunity – before the deadline!"

You need to practice your questions. You need to be comfortable with the words you choose. If you're uncomfortable with the word "buy," don't use it. Instead, say, "When you *own* this …"

Principle:

Ask questions to discover what's in a person's heart and flow with what you learn.

Power Questions:

What questions are you comfortable asking? What words would help you? What words are you better off avoiding?

20

Show Your Personal Brand

Who do you trust? Which company do you trust? What brand of car do you feel is reliable? Persuasion is very much about trust and credibility. A personal brand is a shortcut to trust. The central idea of a personal brand is to answer the question: "What are you best known for?"

Persuasion Master: Orville Redenbacher

Orville Redenbacher* created an innovation – a new type of popping corn that popped much fluffier than standard popcorn. He engaged a branding company, and they advised that Orville become the brand. It was *Orville Redenbacher's Gourmet Popping Corn.* Orville, through visual effects, continues to star in commercials for his terrific product.

Here is another example of a personal brand: *Tom Marcoux, America's Communication Coach.* We know that the central idea

....
* Along with his partner Charlie Bowman.

of a personal brand is to answer the question, "What are you best known for?" For example, to illustrate how I help clients impress audiences, prospective customers, and others, I use the phrase: *When you need to make them go "Wow!"*

As I mentioned in a previous chapter, these are the five elements of your personal brand:

1. The answer to the question, "What are you best known for?"

2. A story that moves emotions

3. A memorable phrase

4. A label

5. A sound bite

A crucial element of having an effective personal brand is *being known as a kind and helpful person.*

To solve the problem of having no contacts, learn the essence of power-networking: *helping people.*

Let's break this down into a pattern for successful networking – to help people you need to be observant. For example, two days ago, my father called to tell me about a segment on the 11 p.m. news entitled "Protect Yourself from Spyware." I watched the segment, took action based on the information presented and called my father to let him know the successful outcome.

1. You observe a way to help a person.

2. You contact the person and give him or her the helpful information.

3. The recipient takes action based on the information.

4. The recipient reports to you on the outcome of the action taken.

Notice that both people do their part. When someone in your network of contacts does you a good turn, be sure to let her know the outcome of the action you took using her information.

A newcomer to an industry may wonder, "What do I have to contribute?" Each person has eyes, ears, and intelligence.

Here's a powerful example – I direct motion pictures. Actors want to be cast in my films. What will help me as a director and producer? Tips on fundraising and distribution! One actress sent me e-mails about fundraising sources and distribution. She was *helping* me. The good news was that this actress was a talented and positive person for the movie set. I subsequently cast her in four productions.

A number of people begin new careers by joining a trade association and volunteering to help with events. As a result, they gain valuable contacts. Be sure to volunteer in ways that represent your skills and talents. This is important, because you will develop a reputation for being both helpful and competent. That's a good personal brand!

Principle:

Your personal brand answers the question: "What are you best known for?"

Power Questions:

What are you best known for? How can you express this through a story that moves emotions, a memorable phrase, a label and a sound bite?

21

Increase Listening

When you're listening, you're creating rapport. Also, you're gaining crucial information with which you will be able to serve the Buyer effectively. You'll persuade her that *you know what's important to her*. That's only possible through listening.

Persuasion Master: Mary Kay Ash

Mary Kay Ash, founder of Mary Kay Cosmetics, created a multimillion dollar organization through the power of team-building. Mary Kay said, "No matter how busy you are, you must take time to make the other person feel important." Listening to a person helps her feel important.

Let's glance at what Mary Kay has accomplished. Mary Kay Inc. is one of the largest direct sellers of skin care and color cosmetics in the world. The company has achieved more than $2.2 billion in annual wholesale sales. The company's independent contractor sales force includes nearly 1.6 million

Mary Kay Independent Beauty Consultants in more than 30 markets worldwide.

The secret is that Mary Kay *helped* the women who started with her company. It is reported that shy women who could not order a pizza learned to express themselves with confidence.

In business circles, Mary Kay has been thought of as one of the most effective persuaders and business leaders of all time. She said, "We treat our people like royalty. If you honor and serve the people who work for you, they will honor and serve you."

To honor a person and make her feel important, we learn the following.

Five Power-Listening Methods

Ask Questions

You can start listening when you have asked a gentle question. I often begin with: "I'm Tom, and you are ...?" Then I ask something like: "So how do you know Eloisa, our host?" or "What's working for you at this conference?"

Stay Silent

Sometimes, we might find it difficult to wait and stay silent while another person pauses to think. The silence can be unnerving. At this point, it can help to repeat quietly in your mind: "I'm listening. I'm building rapport. He is thinking. That's good. I am being supportive."

Voice Reflective Replies

A reflective reply shows the person that you are really listening to and understanding what he or she says. You're like a clear pool of reflective water. Here are some reflective replies:

> "It sounds like that was frustrating to you."

> "That sounds like a tough situation. What happened next?"

Ask, "So What's Your Plan?"

Asking the question "So what's your plan?" implies that the other person is competent. It's also a good way to avoid reflexively "rescuing" someone, that is, solving a person's problem for him. This question gives you another opportunity to keep listening.

Ask, "Would You Like Me to Brainstorm With You or Just Listen?"

Certain individuals have the annoying habit of trying to solve problems, even though the person in front of them has not asked for help. Often, the person just wants to vent his or her feelings a bit. Asking this question helps you understand how the person feels about the situation and how you can be helpful.

Principle:

When you're listening, you're building rapport.

Power Question:

What reflective replies do you want to practice so that you're ready to provide supportive listening to a person?

22

Organize Personaltainment Branding™

Ｈow do you get a Buyer to know you and trust you quickly? Use Personaltainment Branding™ (which I introduced in my book, *Wake Up Your Spirit to Prosperity*). This is the process of connecting with your prospective customers so they trust you quickly – and purchase what you offer. The process involves the P.E.C. Triangle: a *personalized, entertaining,* and *connecting* triangle of material. The P.E.C. Triangle is the basis of effective persuasion skills.

Persuasion Master: George Lucas

George Lucas wanted a studio for his production of *Star Wars*. He needed the tools to *persuade well*, so he commissioned Ralph McQuarie to produce paintings that included images of Darth Vader in a lightsaber battle against his opponent. The images were so effective that Alan Ladd, Jr., then head of 20th Century Fox Studio and its Board of Directors, agreed to the multimillion dollar budget for the first *Star Wars* feature film. The images were *entertaining* (a good idea since it was a feature film), and because they inspired emotion, they were also *connecting*.

George Lucas said, "Dreams are extremely important. You can't do it unless you imagine it." We will add, "And you *can* do it by translating your imagined idea into something that people can see, hear, or feel; thus, you engage their emotions."

In my book, *Wake Up Your Spirit to Prosperity*, I introduced the following vital questions that help the Effective Persuader serve the Buyer.

Five Personaltainment Branding™ Questions

1. What about this is working for you? (*personalized*)

2. When did this become fun for you?* (*entertaining*)

3. What's most important about this for you? (*personalized*)

4. In order for you to know that you have what you want, what has to happen? (*connecting*)

5. How can we make this work better for you? (*connecting*)

When you receive answers to these questions, you have a roadmap toward gaining a sale or cooperation.

• •

* Another version of Question 2: "When could this become fun for you?"

Principle:

Effective persuasion includes providing material that is personalized, entertaining, and connecting.

Power Question:

How can you present material in ways that are personalized, entertaining, and connecting?

23

Nurture Trust

The Effective Persuader learns the methods to gain people's trust as soon as possible. The secret is to take action so people see you as a *trusted advisor*. Trust is a fragile thing. It can take years to build trust, and you can lose it in one minute. Be sure to do everything so people can see how trustworthy you are.

Persuasion Master: Mother Teresa

Many people, regardless of their personal spiritual path, have told me that they felt that Mother Teresa was *genuine.* Let's recap some of what Mother Teresa accomplished. She was persuasive regarding her mission. A winner of the Nobel Peace Prize, she founded the Missionaries of Charity with over 4,000 sisters, an associated group of 300 brothers, and over 100,000 lay volunteers. These people operated 610 missions in 123 countries that included hospices and homes for people with HIV/AIDS, leprosy, and tuberculosis; soup kitchens; children's and family counseling programs; orphanages; and schools.

A friend said, "When Mother Teresa died, she had two saris and no regrets."* The point is that when people knew that Mother Teresa only had two saris, they did not hesitate to donate funds. They trusted her to get the funds to the poorest of the poor so they would be helped.

To be a trusted advisor, follow Mother Teresa's advice: "Let no one come to you without leaving better."

One of Mother Teresa's appealing traits was her lack of ego-centeredness. Mother Teresa said, "I am a little pencil in the hand of a writing God who is sending a love letter to the world."

Trust Begins With Keeping Agreements

Multimillionaire Jack Canfield (cocreator of the *Chicken Soup for the Soul* series of books and coauthor of *The Success Principles)* emphasizes, "Keep Your Agreements." He points out that people who don't keep agreements lose trust, respect, and credibility with customers, friends, and family. Jack offers these tips for keeping your agreements:

1. Make only agreements you intend to keep.

2. Write down all the agreements you make.

3. Communicate any broken agreement at the first appropriate instance.

4. Learn to say "no" more often.

••••••••••••••••••••••••••••••••

* A sari is the robe-like Indian garment that she customarily wore.

To persuade effectively, you must be seen as outstandingly trustworthy and credible. The start of trust is truly seeking to serve others. Mother Teresa said, "Every time you smile at someone, it is an action of love, a gift …, a beautiful thing."

Principle:

Effective persuasion begins with a person trusting you.

Power Questions:

How can you help people see you as trustworthy? What small promise can you make and definitely follow through on?

Conclusion of Part III

You now have tools embodied in the 10-point P.E.R.S.U.A.S.I.O.N. Process.

P – Prepare

E – Emotionalize

R – Reveal Benefits

S – Set Up Similarities and Participation

U – Unleash Stories

A – Ask Questions

S – Show Your Personal Brand

I – Increase Listening

O – Organize Personaltainment Branding

N – Nurture Trust

When you're skilled with positive persuasion, you live on the QuickBreakthrough Level. Why? Because you experience so much less resistance in your life. People want to cooperate with you and help you fulfill your goals.

As I have mentioned: the Einstein Factor Secret revolves around his quote: "You cannot solve a problem on the level in which it was created."

When you're a skilled, positive persuader you float above the level of push and shove in which people often struggle to be heard. Now, you make people feel at ease.

The path of positive persuasion requires lots of practice. And it's worth every minute.

Part IV will open a new vista of possibilities for you. You'll learn the extraordinary advantages of flowing with nonresistance, nonjudgment, and nonattachment. When you rise to this level, you'll experience a delightful ease on your path of more success and fulfillment.

Let's move forward.

Part IV

24

Secrets of Being Unstoppable

Nonjudgment, Nonresistance, & Nonattachment

Who can stop you like no one else? The answer is – yourself. To truly have a *Nothing Can Stop You year*, you need to overcome ingrained patterns that have been instilled by years of conditioning by parents, one's culture, and the media.

> *If you want to be rich, you cannot be normal.*
>
> NOAH ST. JOHN

First, we need to identify what holds many of us back. We need to step away from the normal level of human awareness. We need to rise to a higher level. As I mentioned earlier, the Einstein Factor Secret includes the truth, "You cannot solve a problem on the level in which it was created."

This following quote provides insight:

> *Nonresistance, nonjudgment, and nonattachment are the three aspects of true freedom and enlightened living.*

ECKHART TOLLE

Media and culture emphasize the opposite with messages like, "Resist, fight – that's the way to be a hero." "Judge everyone as less than ideal. Judge yourself as less than ideal." "Buy this and finally your life will be complete."*

Stop! In this section we will take a break from standard patterns of thinking. We'll explore new ways to move forward. For example, inappropriate attachment can slow you down.

We will discuss the benefits of using nonresistance, nonjudgment, and nonattachment in our interactions with others. And we will focus on *being* unstoppable.

Let's begin with nonresistance, since resistance can stop a harmonious interaction right from the beginning.

. . . .

* A commercial perspective infuses much of media and culture. The advertising that forms the core of this influence centers on the premise that one needs to buy something to improve an implied deficiency in oneself or one's condition.

25

Nonresistance

I once learned a particular aikido move that required me to parry an oncoming punch with nonresistance, which is different from how I was trained. I had come from a background of using a traditional karate block when a punch was thrown at me during karate sparring. When forearm meets forearm, there is pain for both people. That is resistance.

Let's face it. Often, one *does not* win by using resistance. On the other hand, in aikido, one just guides the punch. You take the attacker in the direction that he or she was going. You don't stand in front – you sidestep. The force goes past you. That is nonresistance.

So, harvest the wisdom of aikido. Instead of being the rock standing against the raging water, be a canoe that flows with the water. We use the F.L.O.W. Process:

F – Focus on something bigger

L – Laugh it off

O – Open the possibility

W – Wonder

Focus on Something Bigger

F Many individuals I have met get caught up in feeling small
L and vulnerable. This slows them down or stops them completely
O from expanding or improving their lives. What stops them?
W The ego. Compared to your true self (or higher self), your ego
is small. On the other hand, your true self is that part of you
that is naturally courageous, brilliant, and connected with the
goodness of the universe. The true self is expansive and bigger.
Focus on it.

Shifting from the ego to the true self takes significant effort.
Your ego is that part of you that is made up of fears, judgments,
and feelings of being small and vulnerable. The good news is
that when you shift from the ego to your true self, you step
forward on a spiritual path that empowers you.

All religions, arts, and sciences are
branches of the same tree.

ALBERT EINSTEIN

*I could not say I believe. I know! I have had the
experience of being gripped by something that is
stronger than myself, something that people call God.*

CARL JUNG

So how can you have an experience of knowing? You need to get
out of your own way. This is how workshops or retreats can be
priceless. They can give you *an experience of knowing.*

Let me give you example. No, let me take you on a brief
journey.

If you are in your home, go to your kitchen or bathroom
sink. Now run the water. Make it pleasantly cool. Place your
hand under the cool, comfortable water.

Do you feel it? Do you *know* it?

You see, writing about cool water is not the same as
experiencing it.

*We live our lives based on what we believe ... the
beliefs that precede our actions are the foundation
of all we cherish, dream, become, and accomplish ...
With few exceptions, our beliefs originate with what
science, history, religion, culture, and family tell us ...
The essence of our capabilities and limits may well be
based in what other people tell us.*

GREGG BRADEN

Gregg's comment inspires me to *choose beliefs* that empower me
to benevolently serve my readers and audience members. For
example, I believe that this book will find people like you that
I can serve. And I believe it will arrive in your hands at just the
right time.

Also, I make sure to have experiences that empower me. When you experience nonresistance, it is likely to be so unusual that it will surprise you. For example, one time I opened my mail and read something very troublesome for my business. But my response surprised me. Instead of feeling like throwing up and being overly concerned about a money-detail, I was ... wait for it ... calm.

What an extraordinary experience.

So, if someone asks me, "Can you be calm in the face of big trouble?" I can answer, "Yes. I know I can."

And when I was in that calm place, a thought occurred to me – *Money is replaceable when you're creative enough.*

How about that?!

Isn't that an empowered stance? Okay, I can grieve about the loss of money. But I can *simultaneously* do something to make things better! And, do you know what I get with that pattern? Hope!

> *True strength lies in submission which permits one to dedicate his life, through devotion, to something beyond himself.*
>
> HENRY MILLER

Henry's comment guides us in how to achieve a life filled with exuberance, fulfillment, and fun – get immersed in something. One of my team members stated her difficulty with the word *submission*. She said that it is inappropriate to submit to a bully, for example. I responded that we're using the word submission in this way – Submit or *give up* your ego so that you can immerse in life. Devote yourself to something beyond yourself – a cause, Higher Power, your family, making life better for someone else.

Often I have felt the thrill of uniting with team members to create something beneficial – a book or movie – for lots of people.

> *There is no coming to consciousness without pain.*
>
> CARL JUNG

Carl's comment is an invitation to us to feel it all. Some of the greatest wisdom that I have gained in life has been part of a painful process. On the other hand, some people seek comfort first, and they seek to duck pain.

Instead, I'm inviting you to seek growth, opportunity, and fulfillment first. This has worked for me so many times. I attempt more things because I am interested in making a contribution and gaining spiritual growth. I have had enjoyable experiences that my parents could not even imagine. I've started and led companies, written books, traveled to various parts of the world, directed feature films, given speeches to top companies, and more. Such adventures involved trying new things and required me to deal with a significant amount of obstacles, disappointments, and sometimes fear. That price is worth it. I have become conscious of how I need to demonstrate courage and persistence in the face of obstacles.

Every year I do something new; some things work and some don't go as planned. Since I want things to be of high quality and benefit others, I find myself deeply concerned. I sometimes experience fear when things seem to take a bad turn. Then I had an idea that would help – *This is Higher Power's book; I'm participating.*

Can you imagine how much freedom and assurance I had when writing this book? I don't allow myself to be choked by writer's block because I trust that I'll be guided to clarity. Also, I work with trusted editors.*

Focus on something bigger than yourself – Higher Power or a mission to make a contribution. When you do, your tendency to resist the process of exploring and enhancing your personal growth becomes smaller.

Principle:

When you focus on something bigger than yourself, your tendency to resist the process becomes smaller.

Power Questions:

How can you remind yourself to focus on something bigger? How can you let go of your ego in favor of devotion to Higher Power or a cause?

••••••••••••••••••••••••••••••••••

* I know writers who are choked by fear and thus do not complete books. My point is that faith can release anxiety, freeing one to take action, which may include utilizing the guidance of professional editors.

Laugh It Off

*I realize that humor isn't for everyone. It's only for
people who want to have fun, enjoy life, and feel alive.*

ANNE WILSON SCHAEF

When I say, "laugh it off," I'm referring to a process of "shaking it
off." Feel the pain, grieve when necessary, and find opportunities
to experience laughter each day. Similarly, author Joel Osteen
often says, "When someone has done you wrong, you need to
shake it off." He invites his audiences to move on, focus on the
blessings they already have, and move to a place of positive
expectations.

A colleague said, "Isn't asking people to 'shake it off' a
callous comment? Like saying, 'suck it up?'" I responded, "This
is the reason that I emphasize, "Feel the pain, grieve when
necessary, and *find* opportunities to experience laughter each
day." I acknowledge that life is tough. And I also know that brief
laughter can give me the renewal to persist through hardship."

*Whenever you have truth it must be given with love,
or the message and the messenger will be rejected.*

MAHATMA GANDHI

Finding a few moments to laugh each day may seem impossible
when confronted with a truly painful situation. I have
discovered that it is often the best, and sometimes the only way,
to find comfort. For example, during the time that I wrote this
book, I was a passenger in a car that was smashed in the rear

by another car. The collision sounded like an explosion. Being a film director, I have heard special effects explosions on my sets. But the sound of impact between the two cars was scary. Worse yet was how my head whipped backward. I didn't know my head could do that and that I could live through it. The pain was intense.

While I was in the hospital for six hours with a neck brace, I found myself calm and sharing humor with the X-ray and CT scan technicians.

At one point, a technician moved my head to place an x-ray plate below my neck. It made my neck hurt!

She said, "How's that?"

I replied, "I wouldn't recommend it."

She laughed, and I chuckled, too.

The point here is to *not* resist the moment. I just accepted the process I was going through. And I sought to make it as pleasant as possible to all involved.

We remember to avoid building up resistance in ourselves.

Nonresistance may be unappealing to some goal-oriented people. They may have the behavior pattern of resisting or raging against the obstacles that come up. Some people tell me that they must resist in order to accomplish their goals.

I find goals helpful. I prefer to *persist* and avoid loosing energy to the reflex of resisting. You see, I also trust that Higher Power will guide me to make the right decisions at the right time. Good decisions are part of the goal-achieving process.

For example, my company holds this mission:

We create encouraging, energizing entertainment, and edu-tainment in joy of contribution because our work enlivens us and outlives us to serve humankind's rise.

How we reach these goals is up to Higher Power's guidance *and* our own plans and flexibility.

When a vendor sends back a proof (preproduction sample copy) of one of my books that looks terrible, I aim to flow with the process. I look for ways to enjoy humor throughout the day, and I avoid letting one disappointment bring me down.

Humor can be a salve as you still move forward toward what you want.

Principle:

Laugh often and well.

Power Questions:

How can you experience laughter everyday? Will you record a funny TV show, see a DVD, or call a friend who is fun to talk with?

Open the Possibility

When we listen first and hear someone out, we create a situation of harmony.

TOM MARCOUX

F

L

O

W

Listening first to the other person opens the possibility that you will learn how to make a situation benefit both of you. Resistance can shut us down to connecting with someone. It can also keep us from entertaining a new idea. Often I have heard relatives say, "No, that won't work." And they're right. It won't work for them *because they won't work it.* Their comment says they are closed to a new possibility.

> *There were no rules for my father Robert Rossellini. It was life. I thought he brought my mother (Ingrid Bergman) so much optimism, so much vitality, and a sense of adventure.*

ISABELLA ROSSELLINI

I had been working extended hours when I heard this, and it inspired me to plan some fun times with my sweetheart. The idea is to be open to the possibility of expressing your spontaneity and connecting with people who are important to you. So, I planned a short vacation in which she and I had joyful times with friends.

> *I was given courage. I was given a sense of adventure and that has carried me along. With a sense of humor and a little bit of common sense, it has been a rich life.*

INGRID BERGMAN

Ingrid's comment was made to reporters who were trying to get her to say how she regretted some of her decisions. Instead, she expressed her feelings about being open to possibilities. Ingrid didn't resist opportunities.

Is There an Appropriate Time to Resist Something?

Yes. In business we find that we must hold firm so that things work out in a fair way. For example, on three occasions I had to stand firm when family members had difficulties with certain merchants. They would get into some trouble and ask me to fix things. One time I had to say to a hotel manager, "That is not acceptable."

I create *opportunities for nonresistance.* In a conflict, I often use the power of language. I ask questions like, "How about we get this done with X or Y?" In this way, I guide the other person by showing my willingness to be flexible. My flexibility started a positive shift; and this inspired the hotel manager to demonstrate some flexibility, too.

So, in business, temporarily resisting includes some flexibility and an openness to new possibilities.

To shift your thoughts to new possibilities, you can use these methods mentioned by my clients:

- I take a deep breath and stretch. I feel better then.

- I say a prayer and ask God for guidance.

- I get up and walk to the water cooler and get a cup of water. By the time I get back, I have new ideas of how to move forward.

When we shift our thoughts and open ourselves to new possibilities, we move beyond the limits of resistance. We step forward into the bright and fulfilling future that awaits our transformation.

Principle:

Find ways to pause, let go of resisting, and open the situation to new possibilities.

Power Questions:

How can you pause and shift your thoughts to new possibilities? Pick a problem that you're currently working on. Write in your personal journal your answers to the following questions:

- What am I really concerned about here?

- How can I drop resistance?

- How can I be flexible?

- Can I offer a this-or-that solution? (Can I say, "How about we do X or Y?")

Wonder

To wonder invites freedom. It invites you to learn something new. You may even let go of a pattern that had previously imprisoned you.

For example, many people resist change in their relationships. They think they know exactly what the other person will say or do. This leaves all the wonder out of the present moment. Also, to think that you have figured someone out places you in a false superior position. This is the essence of judgment that we'll discuss in the next section.

> *Arguments are caused by two people racing to occupy the victim position in the relationship ... Criticizing and blaming are like being in a hypnotic trance.*
>
> GAY HENDRICKS

Gay's comment invites us to substitute wonder for the habits of arguing, defaulting to a victim-position, and falling into the trance of criticizing and blaming.

Our true freedom is expressed when we open our awareness to new possibilities. It all begins with *I wonder.* Here are examples:

- I wonder how we'll avoid an argument this time and really listen to each other.

- I wonder what I'm really upset about, or if I'm just criticizing my spouse over something trivial.

Some people seem to be quickly and habitually labeling many things as "bad." Here is another view:

> *All the adversity I've had in my life, all my troubles and obstacles, have strengthened me ... You may not realize it when it happens, but a kick in the teeth may be the best thing in the world for you.*
>
> WALT DISNEY

Many of the extraordinary things that Walt Disney and his team accomplished were done when they *wondered* how to solve various problems.

It's kind of fun to do the impossible.

WALT DISNEY

To wonder is to gain access to a source of strength. You can wonder what your current problem or situation is preparing you for. Some of my clients hold the belief that Higher Power trains them for their later great accomplishments.

Great [people] are they who see that the spiritual is stronger than any material force, that thoughts rule the world.

RALPH WALDO EMERSON

We can ask these questions in our own thoughts – I wonder how this helps me grow as a spiritual being. How does this strengthen me?

Principle:

Start with "I wonder about …" and you open yourself to the freedom to discover new and empowering facets of life.

Power Questions:

How can you shift your thoughts so that you connect with the present moment and discover something to wonder about? What is a problem that you're concerned about? Who can you talk with about the details you wonder about? Perhaps you'll say, "I wonder where I can get advice about this. I wonder who can help me with this. I wonder if I'll find a solution in the morning if I get some rest and more sleep."

26

Nonjudgment

We should not pretend to understand the world only by the intellect. The judgment of the intellect is only part of the truth.

CARL JUNG

Adopting an excessively critical perspective is a habit that can deny you much enjoyment and fulfillment in life. It is like a door that slams shut automatically. As Carl's comment implies, many of us may believe that our intellect holds all the answers. This denies us the power of intuition. Also, a number of people feel that human beings can access Higher Power's guidance.

The most beautiful thing we can experience is the mysterious. It is the source of all true art and all science. He to whom this emotion is a stranger, who can no longer pause to wonder and stand rapt in awe, is as good as dead: his eyes are closed.

ALBERT EINSTEIN

We cannot get to the "mysterious," as Albert suggests, if we allow intellectualism to shut down our feelings, intuition, and empowering thoughts.

A Life Affirming Difference

I have repeatedly heard friends and audience members say things like, "Judgment is important. That's how I learn from the past, so I won't make the same mistakes again."

On the surface, this makes sense. And, yet, for those of us who want to experience more times of fulfillment, inner peace, and expanded success, there is an alternative.

To foster the optimal mindset, I recommend substituting the word *discernment* for judgment.* To be a "discerning person" implies flexibility, acceptance, and calmness. To be a judgmental person implies rigidness, defensiveness, and superiority.** Discernment is a softer process that still allows for recognizing that a past behavior did not give you what you wanted so you can choose to act differently in the future.

• •

* The English language is a living entity. At the moment, a number of authors are writing about discernment and judgment, advocating for the adoption of a distinction between the two terms, along the lines advocated here.

** To further support the idea of using the two words differently (discernment and judgment), consider commentary on how the word judgment can function ambiguously. Rick Porritt observes that two different Greek words were originally used in the Bible, but translated into English as one – judgment. He discusses an occasion in Luke where the Greek word contains the idea of "condemning" (which is therein frowned upon). On the other hand, on an occasion in Corinthians the Greek word means "scrutinizing" (which is therein approved of). *To Judge or Not to Judge?: Judgementalism & Discernment*, Rick Porritt.

On the other hand, judgment as personified in judgmentalism includes the dominating acts of the courts, who use judgments as instruments of force to silence opposing viewpoints. Whatever value this has to litigation, this process can cause havoc in our spiritual lives.

So right now, consider adopting the process and attitudes of discernment.

Because, once one acts like a judge, pronouncing one truth, one becomes blind to alternative viewpoints. For example, I had two clients, Matt and Kaya, a couple in the throes of a devastating argument. As an impartial third party, I could see that they were *both* right in a way. But they had already rendered their judgments about one another. Their rigid judgmentalism threatened their relationship.

Instead, they could have discerned what was working or not. They could have recognized that they were both good people with different perceptions and priorities. That would have been a good foundation for resolving their differences.

Therefore, I invite you to adopt the flexible stance. Though it's easier to default to judgmentalism, discernment is more enriching, bringing us access to *all the viable viewpoints*. We *avoid* elevating ourselves to a superior position.

> *Your task is not to seek for love, but merely*
> *to seek and find all the barriers within*
> *yourself that you have built against it.*
>
> RUMI

Indeed, some of my friends have said that, during moments of arrogance, the universe took them down a peg or two. For example, one speaker I know was being abrupt with people because, she said, she was "so busy and in demand." Then one of her best clients suddenly dropped her services. She learned that bringing kindness to people is as important as bringing intellectual solutions.*

To practice nonjudgment, we use the B.E.—H.E.R.E. Process:

> B – Breathe
>
> E – Enter with a benefit
>
> H – Help
>
> E – Energize
>
> R – Respond
>
> E – Engage

Breathe

B
E
•
H
E
R
E

> *When I dare to be powerful, to use my strength in the service of my vision, then it becomes less and less important whether I am afraid.*
>
> AUDRE LORDE

Judgment can be a reflexive response to what we're afraid of. At various times in my life, I have used deep breathing techniques to deal with fear and discomfort. Deep breathing has helped me feel strong. For example, I once had to negotiate with some people who acted in a mean and uncooperative manner. To put

••••••••••••••••••••••••••••••••
* See also the testimony of Gay Hendricks on page 253.

it simply, I felt at a disadvantage and I was angry and afraid of losing. Deep breathing helped me to calm down. Cool water helped, too. I made sure to take some time to be out of the room and away from the opposition.

With deep breathing and calming down, I had the ability to step away from making instant judgments. It helped me realize that my opponents were also afraid of losing. When I returned to the room, I was able to propose a solution that demonstrated my flexibility. My movement off my own position invited my opponents to alter their position a bit. We were then able to complete the transaction in a way that both sides saved face and gained something valuable.

For years, as an instructor of Comparative Religion to college students, I have noticed how a number of spiritual paths emphasize breathing, prayer, and movement. When I teach deep breathing at a spiritual bookstore, I often guide the audience through the *Breathe in God Process*. I ask, "Do you feel vulnerable or small? Would you like to feel connected to the goodness of the universe? Would you like to feel B.I.G. – that is, the Breathe in God Process."

Breathe In God

> **Step 1:** Breathe in and allow your belly to inflate while simultaneously saying in your mind: "God"
>
> **Step 2:** Hold your breath for one second.
>
> **Step 3:** Breathe out while saying in your mind: "Thank you."

During my workshops, I have the audience include movements from tai chi and yoga as they breathe in "God." If you're interested, a number of DVDs related to tai chi and yoga are available at your local store or via the Internet.

> *If the only prayer you ever say in your entire*
> *life is thank you, it will be enough.*
>
> MEISTER ECKHART

Principle:

Breathe deeply and calm down in order to quiet judgments and open the door to new possibilities.

Power Questions:

Think of a time when you were in an uncomfortable situation. Can you imagine how first doing some deep breathing would have helped you slow down, calm down, and gather your thoughts? Imagine your next challenging situation – How can you step away, do some deep breathing, and then return with new energy?

Enter With a Benefit

When you make a judgment about something or someone, what do you really want? Do want to help the situation? Do you want everyone involved to feel better or gain something of value?

Enter with a benefit. That is, shift your thoughts from merely standing up for your rights to ensuring benefit for all involved.

The problem with judgment is that it puts you into a false superior position, like saying, "That's no good." But the difficulty with this approach is that we often discover later that our perception was off. And even if you keep your judgment as a silent thought in your mind, people can still feel it. They can pick up the subtle cues in your face and body language. One of my team members said, "Judging can be like a mirror. When I judge, I get impacted by other people's negative judgments." It's similar to when we hear that someone doesn't like us; we can have the tendency to dislike that person in return.

> *The meeting of two personalities is like the contact of two chemical substances: if there is any reaction, both are transformed.*
>
> CARL JUNG

Sometimes, judgments seem perfectly rational, and we have judgmental thoughts by reflex. One time a friend was, in effect, hiding from the truth. My mind jumped to this thought:

> *People who live with their head in the sand get kicked in the butt.*
>
> TOM MARCOUX

In the moment, making this comment might help someone, or merely get the person angry. Again, a judgment sounds like the speaker is putting him or herself above another. That does *not* inspire connection.

So how do we do this nonjudgment thing?

First, take a moment, breathe deeply, and ask yourself – Is there any chance I could be off about this thing? Am I perceiving this in a way that I may be missing something?

What jumps into my mind is a time when my perception was significantly off. I was 17 years old when my first love relationship ended, and I felt horrible. Later, I learned something troublesome about my former lover. I looked skyward and said, "Thanks for saving me from that one!"

To enter with a benefit requires that we have space to take in what is going on in this moment.

When we feel trapped, we can scratch at someone like a cornered animal. To feel trapped or upset usually involves some form of judging. We feel that someone is doing something that is unfair to us. In fact, we need to feel some form of freedom. We need freedom from our own pain that is expressed as judgments.

So where is your true freedom?

Would you join me in this present moment with the idea that we may *not* clearly perceive where our true freedom is?

The shoe that fits one person pinches another; there is no recipe for living that suits all cases.

CARL JUNG

A number of spiritual paths invite us to approach life with humility. And it may surprise you that humility actually gives people an experience of true freedom.

I coined a phrase *healthy humility*, which includes having an appropriate sense of our place in the universe. We are beings connected with others. We have worth and value, and a human perception that can be limited in the moment.

> *The moment my attitude of cheerful humility slips into self-righteousness or arrogance, the universe will just as cheerfully step in with an unexpected way to make me humble again.*

GAY HENDRICKS

Judgment is not a humble stance toward life. In striving for humility, seek to open your awareness. Look for ways in which a challenging situation can benefit everyone involved. Silently ask yourself, "How may I serve here? How can I take action so that everyone, including me, feels better and receives value?" Carry a notebook and quickly jot down the ideas that arise. You'll be glad that you did.

Principle:

Open your awareness and discover ways to benefit others.

Power Questions:

How can you shift the direction of your thoughts? Can you silently say, "He's a human being. How can I help him feel that he will win and do well in this situation?"

Help

> *It is time for parents to teach young people early on*
> *that in diversity there is beauty and there is strength.*
>
> MAYA ANGELOU

How can you quickly feel secure and connected with the goodness of the universe? Help someone. First, we need to acknowledge the value of diversity, and that our perception in the moment can be off. We really do not know what is best for another person. People are different in their preferences and their true needs. That person may need to go through some tough times to learn lessons for future situations.

Although we may want to help someone, that person may resist. When this happens, he or she is forging a personal path. For this reason, I often ask, "How can I be supportive of what you're doing?"

> *Success is achieved by developing our strengths, not by*
> *eliminating our weaknesses.* *
>
> MARILYN VOS SAVANT

• •

* This quote is about the value of finding one's best talents and devoting energy there. But it overstates the point. For example, one of my clients is best served in hiring a great illustrator instead of improving his meager cartooning skills. Some weaknesses can be career-crippling. So careful self-evaluation is critical in balancing attention between skills and weaknesses and deciding which to address.

Imagine how much good will you can inspire in someone when you are supportive and help the person experience her strengths.

With audiences, I mention that I'm a recovering Mr. Fix-it. So, now I ask, "How can I be supportive of what you're doing?"

Principle:

Honor the fact that each person is on a different path. Ask, "How can I be supportive of what you're doing?"

Power Questions:

Remember a time when someone close to you was angry or emotional in some way. Did you react inappropriately? Did you pause and offer support? Are you a person with a spiritual focus who likes to say a silent prayer before an interaction? If so, consider this simple prayer, "How may I help?" If a spiritual path is not of interest to you, consider envisioning positive outcomes before you interact with the other person.

Energize

Judgment hurts us because it often drains our energy. As soon as I have a negative judgment, I can feel my eyebrows scrunch up in tension. Instead, I'd rather flow in each present moment.

I Don't Want to Play That

I recently talked with a relative who started complaining. My spontaneous response was, "I don't want to play that." This came up because I had been doing some research on entrainment. Entrainment is when we sync up with a rhythm. I know that when I feel tired, I can play certain songs that will lead me to perk up and resonate to their beat. I feel energized!

So when I thought, "I don't want to play that", I was thinking that I didn't want to play a "complaining song." Another way to look at it is, "I don't want to play that beat (or game)."

To avoid going into a downward spiral with my relative, I asked, "Oh, would you like to hear something on the radio?" We were traveling in a car. A cheerful song lifted the mood. We have all witnessed the downward spiral of someone in a bad mood. For example, I remember a time in high school when a football player was in a bad mood and started a fight with me. He continued to get in trouble with his teachers that day.

The solution is to pre-plan your responses so that you can, almost by reflex, do something healthy to lift your mood. Choose, ahead of a tough time, what you would like to entrain to. My clients choose to take a brief walk, get a drink of water, listen to uplifting music, or play with a family pet. It's up to us to choose what we entrain to.

I avoid watching televised news broadcasts before I go to sleep. This guards my dreams from being disturbed and turned into nightmares. I prefer restful and renewing sleep. Some researchers state that nighttime television viewing adversely affects one's pineal gland.* We note that the pineal gland

••••••••••••••••••••••••••••••••••

* "Melatonin is a natural hormone that your body uses to regulate sleep cycles. Melatonin is triggered by exposure to light. The natural rhythms of the day are regulated by the pineal gland in what is called Circadian rhythms. ... at least one hour before sleep, turn off the television, dim the

produces melatonin, a hormone that affects the modulation of wake/sleep patterns.

To energize is to make good choices about sleep, nutrition, exercise, and avoiding "downers." I have found that certain cartoon strips that emphasize complaining sap my energy. It took repeated requests for me to get an old friend to stop sending me certain cartoons via email. Without exposure to those cartoon strips, my energy is protected and enhanced. I invite you to take similar action to avoid the downers in your life.

This book is about your *nothing can stop you year.* Enhance your energy so you have the ability to press on through obstacles.

Principle:

Pay attention and choose empowering energy to focus on.

Power Questions:

What are the forms of downers in your life? Do certain activities, people, TV shows or other forms of media bring down your energy? How can you avoid the downers that are both inside and outside of yourself? How can you enhance your own energy?

. . . .

lights, and prevent exposure to bright lights. This will begin the trigger to your pineal gland that night is setting in. Lights with less of the blue color are also helpful, as they do not suppress melatonin." Melanie Grimes, adjunct faculty member, Bastyr University.

Respond

Someone cuts you off in traffic. Do you respond or react? Many of us will silently answer, "I react with anger. I mean, someone could have been killed!"

Judgment often happens when we take a spit-second jump into the past – into our past feelings, our past theories, and our past thoughts. We can jump to a belief like, "People who cut off others in traffic are ignorant [insert angry word here] who should have their licenses taken away!"

Here's something interesting – I started feeling irritable when I typed the above words. This is the problem with judgments – they raise our negative or irritable feelings to the surface. Judgments are connected to beliefs.

Beliefs are often about the past. We believe things follow a pattern. We can make determinations about something based on our *perception* of what happened before. As I mentioned earlier, our perception in the moment can be off track.

Some people talk about how they cannot get a break. The truth is the past does not determine the future. You can make *a new decision today* that will alter the course you are on. It's as simple as the course correction that a pilot makes on the way to Hawaii. So, to enjoy life, we want to learn to respond in a positive way and *not* merely to react to something.

In my book, *Secret Influence to Get You Out of Trouble*, I wrote about how I restrained myself from reacting to my father after he cut off communication with me. I could have reacted negatively and expressed my pain with letters that attempted to "straighten him out." That just would have added fuel to the fire.

Instead, I chose to respond positively and found a different way to connect with my father. I sent him a happy-looking card that depicted Kermit the Frog playing the banjo.

I wrote:

> *Dad,*
> *Happy today. Thank you for holding me to high standards. This has made my life better.*
> *Love, Tom*

My heartfelt comment helped my father feel better. Soon we were again talking on the phone and meeting in person.

Have the courage to act instead of react.

OLIVER WENDELL HOLMES

If I had followed suit with my father's unfortunate example, the situation could have turned into a grudge or a feud. When someone feels badly, delays in communication can lead them to become thoroughly entrenched in their own opinions and points of view. It becomes even more painful to loosen up and become less rigid.

Consider this old spiritual phrase, "Would you rather be right or happy?"

Apparently, when we look around at this world, numerous individuals prefer to be right – to the point of war and other horrible outcomes.

From this moment forward, let's choose to find ways to *respond* rather than to react to uncomfortable situations.

How Can You Respond Instead of React?

It's as easy as 1-2-3:

1. Breathe

2. Observe

3. Shift

Breathe

Breathing deeply is the first step to calming down so that you do not react immediately. You can say a prayer in your mind, like, "Higher Power, please help me calm down now."

Observe

Researchers note that people who meditate daily develop the ability to connect with their Observer.* The Observer is that part of you that can calmly look at your ego getting upset and say, silently, "Oh, there I go again."

When would it help you to flow to the Observer? Anytime you feel upset. My clients have mentioned frustrating times while driving, waiting in a long line, being placed on hold, or when a colleague rants on and on. At these times, the Observer can focus on calming behaviors like deep breathing, taking a walk, or drinking some cool water.

••••••••••••••••••••••••••••••••

* "Harvard Medical School instructor Sara Lazar [discovered] people who meditate 40 minutes a day have 5 percent thicker brain tissue in the parts of the prefrontal cortex that ... handle emotion regulation, attention, and working memory, all of which help control stress." Amanda Ripley, *The Unthinkable: Who Survives When Disaster Strikes – and Why.*

Shift

To shift, use a physical movement. For example, I sit down when I feel agitated. I recall having a heated conversation with my sweetheart. I sat down on the stairs. As she started to move away from me, I shifted to a lower stair. In this way, I descended, following her to the garage.

> *Fear grows in darkness; if you think there's a bogeyman around, turn on the light.*
>
> DOROTHY THOMPSON

Judgment can be a form of darkness. We have only our own perceptions to go with. We need to make space for the light of new ideas. As you can see, I enjoy quotations. The great writers and thinkers inspire me to see the world anew.

Principle:

Practice pausing before responding. When you do, you will avoid the loss of energy and time from inappropriate reactions.

Power Question:

How can you pause in order to give you the time you need to consider how to respond positively?

Engage

Many of us feel bad more often than we would care to admit. I have certainly gone through tough patches in my life.

Upon reflection, I realize that my focus had at times been in a downward direction. The key to avoiding this is to actually write down your repetitive negative thought patterns. Have you noticed yourself thinking things like, "I could lose my job if I don't get this right." "My spouse just doesn't care anymore." "No one understands the stress and pressure that I am under."

Sometimes negative statements like these can have a tinge of truth, and it may be necessary to consult a counselor or coach to make improvements. However, the important distinction is to identify what you *can* do and what you truly *cannot* control. Know when you are caught up in an obsessive and destructive cycle of brooding with the same repetitive thought patterns.

To *engage* with this present moment, we need to release ourselves from brooding. Because I wanted to feel better and get more done, I learned to effectively change my focus by carefully choosing the questions I ask myself.

Let me show you the difference between a destructive question and a good question.

> **Destructive questions:** Why does this always happen to me? Why can't I get what I want?
> **Good questions:** What am I learning here? How can I do better next time?

> *The answer is in the question. Ask better questions. How does this help me grow as a spiritual being?*
>
> TOM MARCOUX

To engage with life in a healthy and productive way – Choose your empowering questions.

I had been pursuing the idea of empowering questions for at least 12 years, and I wrote about them in seven books.

Then, just this year, I came across a book by Noah St. John entitled, *The Secret Code of Success*. In this book, Noah describes what he calls "afformations," which he says are better than affirmations. Noah writes, "We are really *forming* new thought patterns, which *form* a new life for us."

Here are a few of Noah's afformations:

- Why am I so happy?

- Why do I have enough?

- Why am I so loved?

- Why am I rich?

What I like about afformations is that the process leads my mind to immediately reply with answers that start with "because." Here are a few of my personal "because" responses to Noah's questions:

- Because I have someone to love, something to do and something to hope for.

- Because I study everyday, I'm finding new ways to help people, resulting in increased income for my company.

- Because I actively live by practicing the virtues of healthy humility, generosity, compassion, and kindness.

- Because I'm surrounded by friends and team members who improve the projects that I begin.

- Because I'm doing things to help people improve their lives, and Higher Power guides me.

When I was earning my degree in psychology, I came across the book by Irvin Yalom entitled *Existential Psychotherapy*. Irvin said that the solution for human dilemmas is *engagement*. We engage or immerse ourselves in life as it is now. We fully devote ourselves to that which is positive and creates connection with other people and even Higher Power.

As I'm writing this, I'm listening to the song "Green Light" sung by John Legend (with Andre 300). The lyrics talk about being ready to go right now. That's in line with engagement. We need to release our distractions and pain so that we can meet each moment with positive energy.

People focused on judgment often do not meet people in this moment right now. They see through a filter of prejudice and beliefs. Instead, let's aim to engage with each person and each moment in this instant. To engage creates connection and puts people at ease.

This is a process. Begin now so you can have a *nothing-can-stop-you* year.

Principle:

Engage and immerse yourself in this moment now.

Power Question:

How can you release distractions and shift your attention to this present moment?

27

Nonattachment

Nonattachment can often feel difficult or impossible to accomplish. When I talk with college students in my Comparative Religion class, nonattachment is a topic that feels strange to many in the room. Certainly, if we're talking about our friends and family, we feel truly attached. But imagine if we had the flexibility or even the softness to not be rigid about what we expect or demand from our loved ones. Unfortunately, it may seem natural to fall back to the pattern of – If you really loved me, you would never raise your voice or slam the door.

Nonattachment is the process of connecting with life as it is now, and *rejoicing for anything that is positive*. For some people, this may be a whole different view of nonattachment. They state that their view of nonattachment is being forced to let go of what they want or it's a process of not getting involved.

Instead, we can use nonattachment in a way that gives us more positive feelings. For example, one of my clients suffered an injury at work. It was then that she realized that she had a choice in each moment. She decided to live each day with fewer negative attachments. And she decided *not* to wait to be happy until after she recovered, which would take two months. She decided to appreciate any moment when her thoughts were not overwhelmed by her physical pain. For example, she soaked in a warm bath and relished the soothing feeling on her legs and torso.

Author Stephen Shapiro talked about "not looking for a specific outcome, but instead [you] are open to any outcome that could be of interest." In this way, one is nonattached to only one outcome. This is a process of backing off from demands in favor of having *preferences*. This is a softer, more flexible, and freer way to live.

In order to fully embrace the experience of nonattachment, we use the L.E.T.—G.O. Process:

> L – Listen
>
> E – Embrace the moment
>
> T – Target Global Metaphors
>
> G – Give
>
> O – Observe

Listen

One way to loosen the grip of judgments and attachments is to *listen first*. Tell yourself, "Listen a moment." We need to notice that there is tension when two people meet – Each person wants to express him or herself first.

When you listen first, you're winning. You're creating harmony and closeness as opposed to space and separation.

True listening is a constant *reapplying* of our attention back to the speaker. When you find that your mind drifts into judgment, you need to refocus on the speaker. Ask a gentle question. Here are examples:

- That sounds frustrating. What did you do next?

- How did you feel when that happened?

- What would you like to do now?

> *Never apologize for showing feeling. When you do so,*
> *you apologize for the truth.*
>
> BENJAMIN DISRAELI

Although Benjamin may be pointing to a useful idea, I also realize that it's sometimes best to practice restraint and avoid expressing negative emotions in response to a speaker's thoughts. I have found it helpful to pause and listen to the other person first. After the other person has expressed herself, she will likely be open to hearing my viewpoint. And by then, I will likely have calmed down to a helpful degree.

Benjamin's comment also reminds me to listen to myself.

> *You are not upset for the reason*
> *you think that you are.*
>
> DR. WAYNE DYER

Wayne is referring to a spiritual concept that has been echoed throughout the centuries. The way to uncover what you're really upset about is to pay attention to your random thoughts and feelings. Capture them in a personal journal, and the process can reveal new insights. You may find yourself saying, "Oh! That's how I really feel about this. Then maybe I should switch gears now and do things differently."

As I mentioned elsewhere in this book, the ego is that part of us that is made of fear and feels small and vulnerable. The secret is to listen to your self. When you do, your ego will not cause havoc. When the ego is heard, it quiets down. That gives you space for nonattachment.

Here's an important distinction – I'm talking about hearing the ego and not necessarily obeying the ego.

> *The only way to tell the truth is to speak with kindness.*
> *Only the words of a loving [person] can be heard.*
>
> HENRY DAVID THOREAU

Being heard is crucial. Your ego wants to be heard. Be kind to your ego by listening to it. Then you can make plans and take action to nurture yourself or get nurturing from people you trust. Practice hearing yourself. I wrote a whole book on the topic, entitled *Be Heard and Be Trusted*, and in it I provide exercises that help you support yourself and to support others.

I want to emphasize that you need to be trustworthy to yourself. When you take care of your own needs, you'll find that you have the surplus energy you need to listen to other people first. And that's the first step to nonattachment. Listen first and avoid making immediate demands. You will then step forward in harmony.

Principle:

Listen first. Pause and make space for a new viewpoint.

Power Questions:

How can you pause and listen? Can you take a time-out and go to your car? Can you take a walk to the water cooler or around the block? Can you ensure that you have the energy to listen? Do you need more sleep, some recreation, or regular exercise?

Embrace the Moment

How can you embrace the moment?

First, you *cannot* do it if you're holding up your hands (metaphorically) and saying, "Oh, no! Take it away! Take it away!"

Here's a place to start – *Find something to appreciate now – this second.*

In this moment, say, "I am grateful for …"

At this moment I am grateful for the opportunity to write. Earlier today I finished grading my graduate students' final projects. Whew! I'm free! Free to do what? Free to write these words!

I'm grateful that you're reading these words. Being helpful to you is part of how I experience fulfillment in my life.

Now it's your turn. Embrace this moment. Let go (remember the L.E.T.—G.O. Process) of clinging to past judgments and expectations. Open your awareness to what *is* working right now.

Principle:

Embrace the moment by focusing on what you're grateful for right now.

Power Questions:

How can you remember what you're grateful for? Will you ask yourself, silently, "What am I grateful for?" Will you write your thoughts of gratitude in your personal journal? How could focusing on what you're grateful for increase your energy to have a *nothing-can-stop-you* year?

Target Global Metaphors

Some years ago when I was directing films, I held this metaphor – In a relationship, each person is like *a bottle of water in a desert*. Each person's good will is finite. Do you realize how scary this is? The bottle implies that the water is limited, and a desert without water is a deadly place.

In recent years I have sought to replace that water bottle metaphor with something more hopeful and healthy.

Now I focus on *Renewable Streams in the Forest*. This new global metaphor guides me to empowering questions like:

- How can I help people around me renew themselves?
- How can I renew myself?
- How can I create an environment that is nurturing?

A forest provides more natural resources, like streams, trees, and opportunities for food.

Now I ask you – How do you make sure that your relationships are like Renewable Streams in a Forest? Jot down any helpful ideas that occur to you in your personal journal.

I've learned to make sure that team members have time and energy to renew themselves. For example, one of my team members is working on his own book. I make sure that he has a number of days off so that he can concentrate on his project. He can then return to working on my projects with fresh and renewed energy.

> *I have treated many hundreds of patients. Among those in the second half of life – that is to say, over 35 – there has not been one whose problem in the last resort was not that of finding a religious outlook on life.*
>
> CARL JUNG

Jung's comment is pointing us in an important direction. Now, imagine that I'm whispering to you. Sometimes that's how we hear a secret. *How can you truly experience a nothing-can-stop-you year?* The answer – Find your spiritual path.

I have friends who are not interested in spirituality, and I appreciate their diversity. But I notice that they hold to their own moral compass. So, in essence, they have a guiding philosophy that supports them in their life's journey. Your global metaphors form a crucial element of your philosophy or spirituality.

Steve Jobs' following comment implies what's at stake.

Your time is limited, so don't waste it living someone else's life. Don't be trapped by dogma – which is living with the results of other people's thinking. Don't let the noise of others' opinions drown out your own inner voice. And most important, have the courage to follow your heart and intuition. They somehow already know what you truly want to become. Everything else is secondary.

STEVE JOBS

The idea is to *not* be overly attached to the approval of others. I invite my graduate students involved with artistic pursuits to set aside some time each week to work on their own personal projects. In this way, regardless of what they will eventually do to earn money, they will find artistic freedom and satisfaction along their life's journey.

Go where your heart leads you. For example, one of my friends is now closing a deal to do a particular project. One year ago she had no idea that doing her own personal project would give her the necessary experience to be a candidate for a paying position. Intuition and Higher Power can guide you through the quiet voice of your heart.

For every beauty there is an eye somewhere to see it.
For every truth there is an ear somewhere to hear it.
For every love there is a heart somewhere to receive it.

IVAN PANIN

One [person] with courage makes a majority.

ANDREW JACKSON

Now it's your turn. A global metaphor is a story you tell yourself that has been encapsulated in a brief phrase. What are your global metaphors?

Do you say to yourself, "It's too late for me." Or, "I'm still breathing. Better things are in store for me."

Write down your global metaphors in your personal journal. Then identify any disempowering metaphors and write a *turnaround metaphor* next to it.

Here are examples:

- Life is tough* ➠ turnaround ➠ Life is vigorous and I'm up for it!

- I'm too old (heavy, whatever) ➠ turnaround ➠ I can use whatever I have at the moment to create what I want

Take this moment. Yes! – this moment – to write for a mere 20 seconds about a global metaphor you hold that may be holding you back. Then write a turnaround metaphor. Consider posting it in many places so you will see if often.

Remember, a global metaphor is a story you tell yourself that has been encapsulated in a brief phrase. Tell yourself an empowering story. Choose your global metaphors wisely because they guide your habits, and habits lead to a destiny.

••••••••••••••••••••••••••••••••••••

* The comment "life is tough" may be more accurately described as a meme. However for the sake of this discussion, I am including memes when I talk about global metaphors. My reasoning is that the position "life is tough" is a global position and it raises certain implications. Some people look on life being tough as a challenge. Others look on it as being completely unfair. The idea of life being an "unfair game" would be viewed more as a global metaphor.

Principle:

Transform any global metaphor that does not empower you.

Power Questions:

How can you transform your disempowering global metaphors? Have you written a *turnaround metaphor* next to each disempowering metaphor? Will you use Post-It notes on your bathroom mirror and in your day planner to remind you of your new turnaround metaphors?

Give

Nonattachment can be challenging when we feel that we've put a lot of effort into being good to someone. We feel entitled to being treated fairly in return. The tough thing is that a person in pain can flail about and say mean and unfair things. At that point, we're called upon to lend more than our fair share of patience. By the way, I want to make it clear that if someone is being abusive toward you – get away from that person! If you need help, do not hesitate to ask for it from a friend or a professional.

Many find it challenging to live harmoniously with family members. It helps to seek to become stronger personally so that we avoid returning negativity with more negativity. For example, if a family member is rude, perhaps we can demonstrate compassion by not yelling back. In this way, we avoid a negative downward spiral.

A number of authors talk about how relationships are where we go to *give,* and not just *get.* Sometimes we think we know what's best for someone else. Humility calls for us to remember that our perception of others may not be accurate. Knowing this, I choose to ask others, "How can I be supportive of what you're doing?"

> *Remember to be gentle with yourself and others …*
> *Care for those around you. Look past your differences.*
> *Their dreams are no less than yours, their choices no*
> *more easily made. And give, give in any way you can,*
> *of whatever you possess. To give is to love. To withhold*
> *is to wither. Care less for your harvest than for how*
> *it is shared and your life will have meaning and your*
> *heart will have peace.*
>
> KENT NERBURN

In the spirit of nonattachment, discover how you can improve your interactions. Step into the Observer part of your thoughts. Ask questions like:

- What do I want here? Patience? I'll give it.
- A second chance? I'll give it.
- Some time to cool off? I'll give it.

> *Give us grace and strength to forbear and to persevere.*
> *Give us courage and gaiety and the quiet mind.*
>
> ROBERT LOUIS STEVENSON

Robert's comment is a prayer to Higher Power. It reminds me that *to give is divine.*

Happiness is not a goal; it is a by-product.

ELEANOR ROOSEVELT

Earlier in this section we talked about engagement as the solution for human dilemmas. Engagement is immersing in life. When talking with clients and audience members, I often hear how people helped others, and then felt their own mood improve – as a by-product.

The basic rule of free enterprise: You must give in order to get.

SCOTT ALEXANDER

Business is ultimately a spiritual path.

GAY HENDRICKS

I have worked with thousands of people during the current economic crisis. Even in this challenging time, I have found that business owners find hope when they focus on how to give first, which starts a positive cycle with their customers.

When we give, we experience joy, and nonattachment flows naturally.

Principle:

Give first and start a positive cycle.

Power Questions:

Imagine that you want to achieve something that you have never done before. Relationships are crucial for new accomplishments. How can you be supportive in your relationships? How can you give? Would you like to ask, "How can I be supportive of what you're doing?"

Observe

All of man's troubles stem from his inability to sit quietly in a room alone.

BLAISE PASCAL

Some people see this quote and say, "What would a person do when sitting alone quietly?" The answer – Observe. Observe your thoughts and learn to step into the Observer – that part of you that is calm. Many people who meditate learn to *observe* their thoughts. The Observer doesn't get upset because the Observer is not identified with only a small part of you.

My background in martial arts has been helpful when I have acted in feature films. At my current age, I do not kick in the manner I did when I was 25 years old. This bothers me.

But it bothers me for only a moment because my Observer kicks in and provides me with the *space* I need to switch the direction of my thoughts.

> *Me:* I don't kick like I did when I was 25 years old. I'm getting older. Things are slowing down.

> *Observer:* Oh, there I go again. Whoa! Stop! What can I be glad about?

> *Me:* I'm glad that I can still kick! And walk! And run! I'm glad that I still feel healthy. I'm glad that it's not all about kicking (a small part of my life). It's really about the journey that I'm on.

In the long run, perhaps it is helpful that we cannot rely on our youthful bodies to be our identities. Life's journey certainly invites us to practice nonattachment. As one of my editors said, "We trade higher kicks for higher wisdom."

> *The truth will set you free. But first, it will piss you off.*
>
> GLORIA STEINEM

So, are you feeling upset? Okay. Write about it for 20 seconds in your personal journal. Observe your angry feelings. Imagine how you are *more* than these particular feelings. You are more than your body, for example. You are a spirit having a human experience. See how you can practice nonattachment to your ego's obsessions.

Nonattachment Opens the Door to Happiness

How? Let's remember Eleanor Roosevelt's comment,: *"Happiness is not a goal; it is a by-product."*

Immerse yourself in life and happiness will show up as a pleasant visitor.

> *Happiness is not in the mere possession of money; it lies in the joy of achievement, in the thrill of creative effort.*
>
> FRANKLIN D. ROOSEVELT

There is only one happiness in life, to love, and be loved.

GEORGE SAND
pen name of Amandine Aurore Lucile Dupin

How do we express love to someone in the moment? We listen! We make a switch from judgment to nonattachment. At times, someone will say something and my fast-moving mind will have a quick retort. But I pause to do the loving thing. I listen and say, "Okay." When I say okay, I mean, "*I hear you and you are valuable to me.*" Sure, I could say something clever, but that just gets me separation – the opposite of closeness.

What we call the secret of happiness is no more a secret than our willingness to choose life.

LEO BUSCAGLIA

Observe your choices. Choose life. Choose to listen and to respond.

That is happiness; to be dissolved into something completely great.

WILLA CATHER

Give yourself opportunities to express your creativity. It takes creativity to do many things in life. You're creative when you can balance work, family, and other activities. You're creative when you nurture yourself and take care of your body through nutrition and exercise. You're creative when you try new activities and, perhaps, discover a new hobby.

> *Generosity is the antidote that balances our tendency to be greedy. Humility is the antidote that softens our arrogance. Vulnerability is the antidote to being overly guarded. Being of service balances our tendency to be self-absorbed. Honesty [integrity] is the antidote to our tendency toward deceit. Willingness is the antidote that softens our stubborn nature. Compassion is the antidote that balances our intolerance. The antidotes transcend our limited 'I' perspective, bringing us back into alignment with our higher selves and into the collective heart.*

> DEBBIE FORD

Debbie's comments are some of the most profound and helpful ideas I have heard. I will now provide questions that can help you switch, in the present moment, toward a spiritual path using the virtues she describes.

1. **Generosity** – How can I be helpful in this situation?

2. **Humility** – How am I part of the equation of this problem? Can I be missing something here?

3. **Vulnerability** – Is this a situation in which I can admit my mistake and show how I'll do better next time?

4. **Being of service** – How can I be supportive of what you're doing?

5. **Integrity** – How can I support my feelings of being whole and act in a way that brings benefit to all involved?

6. **Willingness** – Am I'm being unnecessarily stubborn? Can I be willing to find a solution that benefits me and the other person? Can I be flexible in some way?

7. **Compassion** – How might the other person be hurting? Can I help somehow? Can I ask, "What would be helpful to you?"

Practice these questions and memorize them so that when you're under stress, your default setting will ask empowering and responsive questions.

> *All happy people are grateful. Ungrateful people cannot be happy. We tend to think that being unhappy leads people to complain, but it's truer to say that complaining leads to people becoming unhappy.*

> DENNIS PRAGER

> *Pointing derisively to others and talking about what you don't want drops your energy and furrows your brow. Talk about the good and what you want. Don't give the bad equal time.*

> TOM MARCOUX

Some years ago, when I was learning about healthy ways of living, I described to a friend how someone I knew was living in an unhealthy way that caused him problems. But then I had an *A-ha! Moment.* Discussing something negative brought down my energy in that moment. And it was not doing my friend any favors either.

I usually avoid giving bad examples, and just emphasize the positive direction I'm aiming for.

Gain Energy to Consistently Focus on the Positive

When you feel a personal energy crisis, the solution is to devote at least six minutes each day to meditation or prayer. Years ago I used to invite people to just grab a spare three minutes. Then I discovered that I needed three minutes just to calm down. Now I devote six minutes for meditation, even when I'm taking a train or plane to a speaking engagement. I call these moments, *the Six-Minute Makeover*. I realize that makeover often refers to a change in appearance. But here we're talking about a *true* makeover – a deep transformation.

Researchers have noted that people who meditate regularly report bringing those moments of tranquility into their daily lives.* They smile more and feel more at ease.

To Express Courage, One Needs Energy

Remember that you can get a boost of energy from the Six-Minute Makeover.

....

* "Psychologists are increasingly seeing the benefits of meditation in easing disorders like depression and anxiety. The Centre for Mindfulness Research and Practice at Bangor University funds research into meditation. 'The research being done at Bangor is looking into the medical benefits of meditation, shorn from any religious beliefs or Buddhist philosophy,' says Martin Wilks, a chartered counseling psychologist who uses mindfulness practices with his clients," writes Esme McAvoy.

One isn't necessarily born with courage, but one is born with potential. Without courage, we cannot practice any other virtue with consistency. We can't be kind, true, merciful, generous, or honest.

MAYA ANGELOU

Being deeply loved by someone gives you strength, while loving someone deeply gives you courage.

LAO TZU

A number of my clients report that the 6-Minute Makeover gives them time with God, who strengthens them. Sounds great to me!

The size of your success is measured by the strength of your desire; the size of your dream; and how you handle disappointment along the way.

ROBERT KIYOSAKI

A daily spiritual practice of meditation or prayer gives you unconditional support. You don't feel alone. Higher Power waits for you to show up for your 6-Minute Makeover.

Strength does not come from winning. Your struggles develop your strengths. When you go through hardships and decide not to surrender, that is strength.

ARNOLD SCHWARZENEGGER

You will likely feel peace during your 6-Minute Makeover. You will have a brief vacation from problems. You will feel and *know* that what you are and what you have is enough – in the moment.

If you realize that you have enough, you are truly rich.

LAO-TZU

Nonattachment opens the door to creating situations that improve on what you have experienced. After going through an ordeal, we often discover that things were *not* as hard as we had feared. Unfortunately, we had been attached to a false expectation. *Instead, approach each new minute as something that has never before occurred.*

For example, years ago, as a sole proprietor, I would always dread doing the paperwork for my taxes. But, when I added a pleasant component, I'd be surprised at how easy the process was. My strategy – energizing music certainly helped uplift my mood.

I now approach projects in the spirit, "This might flow easier than I expect. I'll just enter each new moment as it arrives."

It is love, not reason, that is stronger than death.

THOMAS MANN

Where does calm energy come from? Your 6-Minute Makeover. I invite you to try an experiment. Pick a certain number of days to experience a daily session of six minutes for meditation, prayer, or quiet time.

An experiment is quiet and gentle. For example, I used the *experiment* method to see if I would add jogging to my daily life. I said to friends, "I'm going to do a 30-day experiment. I'm going to run for ten minutes each day to see how I like it." That experiment was successful and I'm still going strong.

Try a Six-Minute Makeover. After a number of sessions, you'll see a difference. It's worth it.

Principle:

Practice going to the place of the Observer. When you do, you'll be able to engage in nonresistance, nonjudgment, and nonattachment.

Power Questions:

How can you shift to the place of the Observer? Does deep breathing help you? Have you tried a 6-Minute Makeover? Do you truly want a *nothing-can-stop-you* year? Are you willing to try something new? Can you reward yourself for your first efforts?

Conclusion to Part IV

Now that we have viewed the processes of nonresistance, nonjudgment, and nonattachment, I have a question for you, "*What are the benefits of these three processes?*"

The answer – saving time and saving energy. Imagine a conflict eases when you back off and do not attempt to force someone to comply with your request. Imagine that you have the energy to listen first. Then you can avoid the default setting of resistance.

When you resist another,
you inspire that person's resistance.

TOM MARCOUX

What is often necessary is to curb our own resistance and shift to pausing and hearing out the other person *first*. Ask a gentle question like, "So how did it feel when …?"

Meanwhile, judgment is one of the biggest forms of resistance. We have covered the F.L.O.W. Process so that you can shift your thoughts and feelings.

The F.L.O.W. Process includes:

> F – Focus on something bigger
>
> L – Laugh it off
>
> O – Open the possibility
>
> W – Wonder

Finally, nonattachment is very helpful, but it takes practice.

> *It is hard to be tolerant of people*
> *who are intolerant of you.*
>
> MARIANNE WILLIAMSON

Marianne's comment reminds me about the practice of nonattachment. For example, I have family members who find some of my actions strange. Even on a vacation day, my practice is to get up, write, and then go for a run. I'll even write occasional notes when traveling. I have learned to be nonattached about whether certain family members show approval for my habits.

Now it's your turn. What in your life bothers you? Note details in your personal journal. Can you imagine how you might let go of demanding certain responses from people? How much more energy would you have if you were practicing nonattachment?

I recall a story author John Gray told about one of his clients, a woman lamenting the poor treatment and neglect she received at the hands of her mother. As her therapist, John Gray guided the woman to realize that she was fortunate to have a kind aunt who acted as her surrogate mother. Eventually, the woman was able to practice nonattachment with her mother's indifference, and she rejoiced in the loving aunt that she had.

So much energy is lost to frustration because we hold expectations about how we want things to go. For example, as my recent birthday approached, friends asked about my birthday plans. I had already decided to make a plan that included space for spontaneity. I said, "I'm going to let things unfold moment by moment."

My target is to feel it all – the joy, the disappointment, the love, and the hope.

Now it's your turn. How much more ease would your life include if you lived moment by moment? Consider the old refrain, "I learned how to predict certain rain; schedule an outdoor wedding."

To practice nonattachment, a person can schedule an outdoor wedding *with a cheerful backup plan* in case rain appears.

Author Mike Robbins has a valuable question:

> *What am I willing to do today to step out in life?*
> MIKE ROBBINS

Mike's comment reminds us to try new things everyday. I invite you to re-read this section on nonresistance, nonjudgment, and nonattachment to find actions that you can place into your day planner and experiment with.

> *[We] defuse stress by hearing our own feelings and needs ... Empathy is emptying the mind and listening with our whole being ... Staying with empathy, we allow speakers to touch deeper levels of themselves.*
>
> MARSHALL B. ROSENBERG

Marshall's comments remind us to hear our own feelings and needs – and take action to support our own energy. We will then have the surplus energy to live with empathy in the moment. Otherwise, if we're stressed out, our minds will be full of worries. Such negative energy can foster an atmosphere of resistance.

I invite you to use the 6-Minute Makeover (meditation or prayer) to empty your mind and ego so that you can be present with others moment by moment. Remember to stay in empathy. When you do, people will find it easier to explore their deeper personal levels with you. This is an enjoyable result that I have experienced over and over.

> *True success relies on the support and buy-in of others. You must understand the reasons why your vision is important, and you need to be able to clearly communicate that importance ... The expectations we exceed today become the seed for new opportunities in the future.*
>
> TONY JEARY

True success can blossom when you practice the processes of nonresistance, nonjudgment, and nonattachment. This is something that "the happiest man in the world," Buddhist teacher Yongey Mingyur Rinpoche, *knows*. Yongey gained that label of happiest man when researchers used fMRI technology to scan his brain.* They discovered that the happiness areas of his brain were *exceptionally* active.

Yongey knows that we need to practice, practice, practice. Eventually, the processes will become part of you, and you will discover success and fulfillment at a higher level. Only then can you truly experience the Einstein Factor Secret – You will be able to solve a problem because you will be *above* the level on which it was created. When you live on this higher level, you can create a *nothing-can-stop-you* year. This is an experience that will bless your life.

The best to you.

Springboard to Your Dreams

Thank you for your attention and efforts.

We have focused on skills so that you can experience a *nothing-can-stop-you* year. When you live the *Einstein Factor Secret*, you attract more opportunies. People cooperate easily with you and make decisions that are favorable to your dreams and goals.

Remember to return to these pages again and again to reenergize yourself. You will get more value each time you review the steps covered in this book – and take action!

Please visit me at TomSuperCoach.com to get free reports and my free e-newsletter, *Success Secrets*. I also work with clients one-on-one in person and over the telephone, and I present workshops and speeches to associations and companies.

On the following pages, you will find special discounts, presentations, and empowering audio programs and books that will help you continue your education and expand your prosperity. The best to you,

Tom

Tom Marcoux
America's Communication Coach
Motion Picture Director & CEO, Tom Marcoux Media, LLC

Special Offer for My Readers

B ring Tom to your company, conference, or church and get a 10% discount on his fee. TomSuperCoach@gmail.com.

Tom's popular topics:

- Be Heard and Be Trusted
- Truth No One Will Tell You
- Nothing Can Stop You This Year!
- Power Time Management
- Double Your Sales in Half the Time™
- 10 Best Kept Secrets of Persuasion Masters
- Wake Up Your Spirit To Prosperity
- Say Yes to Yourself: Reduce Stress and Increase Ease
- Empower Your Personal Brand

To view a downloadable page of these topics, go to:

bureau.espeakers.com/simp/viewspeaker5261&multimedia

Don't miss a special offer for readers of *Nothing Can Stop You This Year!* at:

www.TomSuperCoach.com/ReaderOffer.htm

Get FREE reports and an e-newsletter subscription, *Success Secrets* (a $195 value!). Also order books and audios, see list at front of book.

Appendices

Glossary

For easy reference, here are listed all the specially defined terms used in this book.

~~~~~~~~~~~~~~~~

12 Elements of the Compelling ⅲ➡ "Compelling, 12 Elements of the"

B.E.—H.E.R.E. Process – It is desirable to avoid passing judgment and thereby looking down on others. Embodying this practice of nonjudgment, is the B.E.—H.E.R.E. Process:

> B – Breathe
>
> E – Enter with a benefit
>
> H – Help
>
> E – Energize

R – Respond

E – Engage

B.E.S.T. Process – To achieve your best year ever, use the B.E.S.T. Process:

B – Build the Castle First

E – Energize

S – Surround Yourself with the Compelling

T – Turn Around Your Moods

Big Picture Forgiveness Process – It takes a process of learning to create forgiveness in our lives in order to help us break free from destructive thoughts. Viewing forgiveness as the big picture allows us to go through the process of letting go of our painful feelings.

1. Acknowledge the pain.
2. Take care of yourself.
3. Examine the situation to gain objectivity from the perspective of a metaphorical helicopter.
4. Become the hero of your own story.

Blessings ➠ "Journal of Victories and Blessings, Daily"

Brand, Personal – This is what makes you unique and trustworthy to your listener. Your personal brand is the answer to the question, "What are you best known for?" The clearly expressed personal brand establishes credibility. It is also part of the process of rising to the QuickBreakthrough Level, on which you have rapport with people and can even get access to their intuition! Here are the six elements of your personal brand:

1. The answer to "What am I best known for?"
2. A story that moves emotions
3. A memorable phrase
4. A label
5. A sound bite

Branding, Personaltainment ➠ "Personaltainment Branding"

Breakthrough Staircase, The – Each year, we have the potential to rise to a higher level. Let's view this process as a staircase. We can rise to Breakthrough 1 this year. Next year, we can rise to Breakthrough 2. Perhaps Breakthrough 3 is a big, flashy breakthrough. But it only happens because we leapt to a new level in previous years. When you use my methods to live on the QuickBreakthrough Level, you experience breakthroughs in your thinking, feeling, and action.

Buyer – This is a generic label to represent anyone you wish to persuade, because you want the person to buy into the ideas, products or services that you're presenting.

Compassion – "Compassion is an antidote that balances our intolerance [and] … transcend[s] our limited 'I' perspective, bringing us back into alignment with our higher selves and into the collective heart." Debbie Ford.

Compelling, 12 Elements of the – When you surround yourself with the Compelling, you automatically go into action. *Also* ⅲ➡ "TriggerSet Method.™" The Compelling includes 12 elements:

1. Your Milestones Binder

2. The inspiring work of the best in your industry

3. Your birthday celebration poster ("the doing now")

4. Books and audio programs that energize you

5. Memorized phrases

6. Project binder with a beckoning cover

7. Your easy, simple process to Keep Score and Achieve More.

8. Your process to Make It a Game You Can Win

9. Daily Journal of Victories and Blessings

10. Power of Alliances

11. Wall of Victory (or poster or corkboard)

22. Specific goal to brighten a loved one's life

Contraction ⅲ➡ "Expansion versus Contraction"

Discernment versus Judgment – As used in this book, an act of Discernment is a flexible, nonjudgmental evaluation, while an act of Judgment is a rigid and/or dogmatic conclusion often imposed from a position of supposed superiority. While this distinction is not part of popular usage, it is established within the arena of positive psychology and opens the door to a life affirming perspective.

Notably, judgment is a habit that denies us the power of intuition and the opportunity for Higher Power's guidance in our lives. *Also* ⟶ "Nonjudgment."

Easethrough – The next evolutionary step beyond a breakthrough. The idea of rising to the QuickBreakthrough Level includes the Easethrough,™ which is better than a standard breakthrough. A breakthrough implies resistance that one must push through. With the Easethrough,™ you neutralize any resistance. Benefits of the Easethrough:

- Save your energy
- Get the pain out
- Eliminate procrastination
- Have more fun
- Enjoy your daily life

Easy Part Start – Identify a situation in which you usually procrastinate. Then use this technique to eliminate pain and eliminate stalling. If you procrastinate about writing because you hate facing a blank screen, call a friend and talk about the report you intend to write. Record your side of the conversation. Then type up your recorded comments. In this way, you eliminate the pain of facing a blank screen.

Momentum breeds momentum. Start with an easy part.

Effective Persuader – The Effective Persuader saves time and gets more done, while eliminating time wasted due to misunderstandings. In the end, this person gets what she wants through the cooperation of other people.

Effort Goal ⮕ "Goal, Effort"

Einstein Factor Secret, The – Albert Einstein said, "You can never solve a problem on the level on which it was created." This means we need to rise to a higher level – the QuickBreakthrough Level. Shifting to the empowered state of the QuickBreakthrough Level gives us heightened awareness and flexibility.

Emotional Leverage™ – This involves using your emotional buttons to move yourself to action. Many people procrastinate to avoid anticipated pain. The strategy is to get the pain out of the situation and thereby eliminate hesitation. That's when you experience an Easethrough.

Expansion versus Contraction – As used in this book, Expansion is a process of opening up to opportunity hopefully, while Contraction is a process of fearfully shutting down. Expansion is the voice of intuition and thus a hallmark of good ideas, contrasted with bad ones. While this distinction is not part of popular usage, it is established within the arena of positive psychology and opens the door to a life affirming perspective.

Expert – An empowering definition of an expert is someone who has devised a system that people like and use.

F.L.O.W. Process – Judgment is one of the biggest forms of resistance. Use the F.L.O.W. Process to shift your thoughts and feelings so as to overcome this resistance.

> F – Focus on something bigger
>
> L – Laugh it off
>
> O – Open the possibility
>
> W – Wonder

For-the-Team Person ⇒ "Team Person, For-the-"

Generosity – "Generosity is an antidote that balances our tendency to be greedy [and] … transcend[s] our limited 'I' perspective, bringing us back into alignment with our higher selves and into the collective heart." Debbie Ford.

Global Metaphors – These are metaphors that capture significant aspects of your world view, also known as "memes." They represent archetypal perspectives. When poorly choosen, they can be paralyzing or otherwise inhibiting.

Your global metaphors form a crucial element of your philosophy or spirituality.

G.O.—N.O.W. Process – To overcome procrastination, we use the G.O.—N.O.W. Process:

       G – Get the pain out

       O – Offer fun

       N – Nurture rewards

       O – Open the pain valve

       W – Wrangle schedules

Goal, Effort – This is a goal defined in terms of the effort required, rather than the result desired. It is a goal harmonized with the perspective that a journey is its own reward. Effort Goals contrast with Result Goals. Effort Goals are much less likely to be met with frustration.

Effort Goals grow naturally from your values; that is, what is most important to you. To help my clients complete their Effort Goals, I coach them to use a Self-Leadership Chart.™

Goal, Impotent – An impotent goal is one prone to failure due to lack of conviction, because (1) they do not have one's deepest desire as a first cause, or (2) they are actually someone else's goal.

Goal, Result – This is a goal defined in terms of the result desired, rather than the effort required. This is most people's paradigm of a goal. Result Goals contrast with Effort Goals. Result Goals can be frustrating, since outcomes are often not within our control.

G.R.E.A.T. Process – *Where does your personal energy come from?* A lot comes from appropriate food and exercise. Use the G.R.E.A.T. Process to improve your energy and your appearance!

> G – Get clear
>
> R – Reform your exercise
>
> E – Empower your eating
>
> A – Align your food
>
> T – Transform the inner you

Great Year Letter – An exercise for visualizing your best year ever. It takes the form of a letter to a confidant about a fictitious past year embodying your hopes for the future.

Higher Power – This is a non-denominational designation for the theist presence in the universe, with no reference to any particular faith. Higher Power as referred to herein has the following characteristics: (1) compassion for the human condition, and (2) concern for the well being of individuals.

Hot Button – In sales terminology, a "hot button" is something that's tied into a person's deepest desires and, sometimes, concerns. When you find out what really excites a person (his or her "hot button"), you make a friend and persuasion becomes much easier.

Humility – In problem solving, humility involves reflecting on the questions, "How am I part of the equation of this problem?" and, "Can I be missing something here?" Debbie Ford writes, "Humility is an antidote that softens our arrogance [and] …

transcend[s] our limited 'I' perspective, bringing us back into alignment with our higher selves and into the collective heart."

Impotent Goal ⟶ "Goals, Impotent"

Inner Child – Our relationship with our inner child is a key to our well being. When we constantly deny ourselves joy, our inner child rebels, and acts out. Remember that the inner child is the part of you that may feel vulnerable or small and that wants to have fun. The inner child is important because it provides the energy you need to improve your life.

Integrity – Synonymous with wholeness, in problem solving, integrity involves reflecting on the question, "How can I support my feelings of being whole and act in a way that brings benefit to all involved?" Debbie Ford writes, "Honesty [integrity] is an antidote to our tendency toward deceit [and] ... transcend[s] our limited 'I' perspective, bringing us back into alignment with our higher selves and into the collective heart."

Journal of Victories and Blessings, Daily – To counteract feelings of underachievement and depression, keep a Daily Journal of Victories and Blessings. In it note down each day's joys and accomplishments, regardless of scale. This will promote feelings of gratitude and blessedness.

Journal, Personal – A vital record of your journey through this book. To get the most from this book, be sure to write down the answer to each exercise in your personal journal as you proceed.

Judgment➠ "Discernment versus Judgment" & "Nonjudgment"

Keep Score and Achieve More – Professional writers keep track of how many words they write each day. These top authors are engaging in a process I call Keep Score and Achieve More. Many authors accomplish their writing goal and then go on to enjoy the rest of day – guilt-free!

The point is to transform making progress into a fun activity. Keeping a daily word-count helps authors feel good and energized as they make progress on a daily basis.

L.E.T.—G.O. Process – In order to fully embrace the experience of nonattachment, we use the L.E.T.—G.O. Process:

> L – Listen
>
> E – Embrace the moment
>
> T – Target Global Metaphors
>
> G – Give
>
> O – Observe

Low Mood First-Aid Kit – This is a toolkit for coping when a crisis snatches away our external sources of happiness. The tools selected are those which connect us with our internal resources for self comfort.

Makeover, Six-Minute – A brief vacation (or quiet time that may include meditation or prayer) from problems that centers you and reaffirms your commitment to nonattachment.

Manipulation – Manipulation is a dark practice where someone selfishly focuses solely on their own benefit to the exclusion of concerns for the listener's welfare. *Also* ⅲ➡ "Persuasion versus Manipulation."

Mastermind Group – A mastermind group is comprised of about six, usually in non-competing enterprises, that regularly meet to help or support each other in their individual goals … Beyond the mere mutual support, in a Jungian sense you also create and tap into a larger mind.

Milestones Binder – In your Milestones Binder, you record the new actions that you take for the first time in the given year.

My clients use a Milestones Binder to experience a new year every year. They use the Milestones Binder to celebrate what they do that is new and different in each year. Your benefits from using the Milestones Binder are two-fold:

1. You give yourself acknowledgement for your dedicated efforts.
2. You gain incentive to stretch, grow and try new activities.

Mission Caption – Some authors emphasize the need to write a mission statement. How many people have memorized their mission statement? Often a mission statement is several pages long.

We live on the QuickBreakthrough Level with the help of what I call the Mission Caption. It can appear like a caption below a photograph. It will help you gain access to your intuition.

Nonattachment – Nonattachment is the process of connecting with life as it is now, and rejoicing for anything that is positive. It is not being forced to let go of what you want nor a process of not getting involved. This is a process of backing off from demands in favor of having *preferences*. This is a softer, more flexible and freer way to live.

In order to fully embrace the experience of nonattachment, we use the L.E.T.—G.O. Process.

Nonjudgment – On the practice of nonjudgment, *see* the B.E.—H.E.R.E. Process. *Also* ⫸ "Discernment versus Judgment"

Nonresistance – Let's face it, often, one does not win by resisting. On the other hand, in aikido, one just guides the punch. You take the attacker in the direction that he or she was going. You don't stand in front – you step aside. The force goes past you. That is nonresistance.

Observer – Observe your thoughts and learn to step into the Observer – that part of you that is calm. People who meditate learn to observe their thoughts. The Observer doesn't get upset because the Observer is not identified with any particular part of you.

Optimal Exercise Chart™ – A tool to help make exercise an I-want-to-do-it part of your busy life.

Pain Valve, Open the – People are more motivated to avoid pain than to gain joy. When stuck, open the pain valve by visualizing a painful scenario that further procrastination will bring to pass and let the this future trauma motivate you to action. This is the second form of Emotional Leverage.™

Persistence versus Resistance – As used in this book, Persistence is is flexible dedication to one's dreams, while Resistance is stubborn adherence to a particular path toward one's dreams. While this distinction is not part of popular usage, it is established within the arena of positive psychology and opens the door to a life affirming perspective.

Personal Brand ⸻➤ "Brand, Personal"

Personal Journal ⸻➤ "Journal, Personal"

Personaltainment™ Branding – This is a powerful technique for structuring your services, interacting with the media, and creating a compelling Web presence. You focus on P.E.C.: personalized, entertaining, and connecting material.

Persuasion versus Manipulation – It is critical to distinguish persuasion from manipulation. For this book, let us make the following distinction:

- **"Persuasion"** is helpful because we start with benefits for your listener in mind.

- **"Manipulation"** is a dark practice where someone selfishly focuses solely on his or her own benefit to the exclusion of concerns for the listener's welfare.

P.E.R.S.U.A.S.I.O.N. Process – Since our focus is on rising to the positive Quick-Breakthrough Level we concentrate on positive persuasion. We will use the ten-point P.E.R.S.U.A.S.I.O.N. Process:

> P – Prepare
>
> E – Emotionalize
>
> R – Reveal Benefits
>
> S – Set Up Similarities and Participation
>
> U – Unleash Stories
>
> A – Ask Questions
>
> S – Show Your Personal Brand
>
> I – Increase Listening
>
> O – Organize Personaltainment Branding™
>
> N – Nurture Trust

Power-Four Questions – These questions are designed to help you get the answers you need to activate you intuition.

> What is your highest leverage?
>
> What is the bottleneck?
>
> How much money? What are other methods?
>
> Can someone else do it?

Power-mations – An affirmation is a statement that positively activates your conscious mind. When you effectively construct the affirmation, you can activate your subconscious mind and intuition as well. To do that, your affirmation needs to be positive, in the present tense, and personal (the 3 Ps).

These improved affirmations are called Power-mations. They are better than standard affirmations because they solve a recurring difficulty of standard affirmations. Some people find that simply saying "I feel terrific" when they clearly do not feel well is lying to oneself. The improvement is to say, "I feel terrific! How? By calling my friend; or by listening to relaxing music …"

A third part of the Power-mation is, "I relax into …" The idea is to allow oneself to flow comfortably with life as it is. You cannot solve some things with action. To feel calm and peaceful, focus on, "I relax into …"

P.O.W.E.R.—M.E.E.T. Process – Now, we will talk about skills for Streamlined Power Meetings. We use the P.O.W.E.R.—M.E.E.T. Process:

> P – Prepare
>
> O – Own ideas
>
> W – Write
>
> E – Engage listening
>
> R – Recognize everyone
>
> M – Mention targets
>
> E – Encourage criteria

E – Enrich efforts

T – Track

The ability to effectively lead Streamlined Power Meetings gives you a true advantage. You can create abundant good will that can lead to breakthroughs!

Power Questions – Power Questions are your inroad to your intuition. Through your intuition, you access a higher level of wisdom and knowledge.

Project Binder – Using a project binder with a beckoning cover is an example of using the TriggerSet Method.™ By working with the binder, we set a trigger. Every time we see our binder, we are likely to go into action.

Qualify Your Thoughts – The idea behind qualifying your thoughts is to respond to any negative thought with the following three thoughts:

1. Don't engage in mischief.

2. Is this a teaching moment?

3. Avoid a downward spiral.

Q.U.I.C.K. Process – Imagine that you could instantly become more insightful and powerful. These advantages are embodied in the Q.U.I.C.K. Process:

Q – Qualify

U – Use Time-Leverage

I – Intuit to Do It!

C – Create (don't compete)

K – Kindle Brand

QuickBreakthrough Level – The empowered state of the QuickBreakthrough Level is one of heightened awareness and flexibility. When you are functioning on the QuickBreakthrough Level, you have the flow of:

- Intuition
- Cooperation
- Connection
- Creativity
- Integrity (wholeness)
- Excellent communication
- Effective action

At the QuickBreakthrough Level, you are free from distraction, pain, worry, limited thinking, judgments, and emotional baggage. You do not procrastinate. On the QuickBreakthrough Level, you have the full use of your resources and skills to gain the cooperation of other people.

React ⮕ "Respond versus React"

Real Power Triangle, The – The following processes are the key to unleashing your real power for boundless effectiveness!

- Questions
- Emotional Charge
- Intuition

Red Alert Weight – A Red Alert Weight is a weight that disturbs you. Getting clear mentally helps you maintain your body weight. When you have a clear goal that works for you as an individual, you are empowered to accomplish your personal goal. One part of this process is identifying your Red Alert Weight and knowing what immediate action-steps you will take if you fall back to your Red Alert Weight.

Respond versus React – As used in this book, a Response is considered and reflective, while a Reaction is unconsidered and reflexive. While this distinction is not part of popular usage, it is established within the arena of positive psychology and opens the door to a life affirming perspective.

Resistance ⟹ "Persistence versus Resistance"

Result Goal ⟹ "Goal, Result"

Science of Emotional Leverage™ – Based on numerous effective processes, the Science of Emotional Leverage is founded on: (1) letting an unhelpful neural pathway fade from disuse, (2) establishing empowering neural pathways, (3) using the TriggerSet Method,™ and (4) replacing undesired behavior. Replacing a behavior and replacing a neural pathway are effective methods for improving your life. A more extended discussion of these ideas is the planned subject of an upcoming book. *Also* ⅢⅢ➡ "TriggerSet Method."

Self-Leadership Chart™ – Clarity helps you feul your progress, and this is motivating. You can use a Self-Leadership Chart to overcome backsliding and replace undesired behavior.

Service – "Being of service balances our tendency to be self-absorbed [and] … transcend[s] our limited 'I' perspective, bringing us back into alignment with our higher selves and into the collective heart." Debbie Ford.

Streamlined Power Meetings ⅢⅢ➡ "P.O.W.E.R.—M.E.E.T. Process"

Teaching Moments – These occur when someone is open to learning something from us. A teaching moment feels like a rare occasion, because many of us are obsessed with our own opinions and perceptions.

When there is no teaching moment, we avoid difficulty by not trying to teach a detail to someone. We avoid gushing advice. We focus on being in the moment, and, often, we do more listening.

Team Person, For-the- – Many of us will do more for family members or friends than for ourselves. If you're this kind of person, you may have found that setting traditional goals for your personal enrichment has not worked. If you set goals that enrich your life plus your family's life, you will find your hidden power.

Time-Delight – Time-Delight is a takeoff on Customer-Delight, which is based on giving something extra and surprising. Make sure that your schedule includes fun and delight to offset fatigue-generating obligations.

Time-Leverage™ – The process of reducing resistance and going into action quickly with the least energy required. In this way, Time-Leverage provides an Easethrough.™ With Time-Leverage, you neutralize your own resistance, a source of procrastination.

Time-Leverage is better than standard time management. Time-Leverage uses your emotions as a fulcrum. That's how Time-Leverage gets you into action. Standard time management, using only a written list, does not give a person the energy to get into action.

T.I.M.E. Process – Many people are natural turtles trying to become racehorses; or owls attempting to be lions. Stop fighting yourself. Use your natural tendencies to your best advantage. Use, the T.I.M.E. Process, part of the Science of Emotional Leverage™:

> T – Target
>
> I – Intensify
>
> M – Minimize
>
> E – Expect

Took Kit of Rewards – To transform your relationship with food, I suggest developing your Tool Kit of Rewards. Reward yourself, increase your comforts, and strive to leave food out.

TriggerSet Method™ – This is a breakthrough process, because we rely on physiology instead of willpower. It goes as fast as:

Eyes see ▬▶ Feeling in the body ▬▶ Action!

For example, I have used the trigger of a portable sign that reads, "Only water 9 p.m. – 6 a.m." This is a positive trigger. It tells me exactly what the healthy thing is to do. It does not dwell on "food" or "hunger pains." When you are thinking clearly, set triggers so you will act automatically.

Victories ▬▶ "Journal of Victories and Blessings, Daily"

Vulnerability – "Vulnerability is an antidote to being overly guarded [and] … transcend[s] our limited 'I' perspective, bringing us back into alignment with our higher selves and into the collective heart." Debbie Ford.

Wall of Victory – This is a bulletin board, corkboard, or the like, upon which you post photos, clippings, notices, etc. relating to your ongoing successes in life. You can also include inspirational mock-ups of a successful future.

Willingness – "Willingness is an the antidote that softens our stubborn nature [and] … transcend[s] our limited 'I' perspective, bringing us back into alignment with our higher selves and into the collective heart." Debbie Ford.

Further Reading

The following list of books and audio programs provides the reader with select landmarks in the rich literary landscape which has informed this book. Enjoy!

~~~~~~~~~~~~~~~~

Adler, Bill *see* Winfrey, Oprah & Bill Adler

Albom, Mitch, *Tuesdays with Morrie: An Old Man, a Young Man, and Life's Greatest Lesson,* 2002, 192p, Broadway, 978-0767905923

Alessandra, Dr. Tony, *Charisma: Seven Keys to Developing the Magnetism that Leads to Success,* 2000, 288p, Business Plus, 978-0446675987

_____, *Non-Manipulative Selling,* 2nd Ed., 1992, 276p, Fireside; 978-0671764487

_____, *The Dynamics of Effective Listening,* 2008, audio, 5 hours, 29 mins, Nightingale-Conant

Alessandra, Dr. Tony & Michael J. O'Connor, *The Platinum Rule: Discover the Four Basic Business Personalities and How They Can Lead You to Success*, 1998, 304p, Grand Central Publishing, 978-0446673433

Allen, Marc, *The Greatest Secret of All: Moving Beyond Abundance to a Life of True Fulfillment*, 2007, 128p, New World Library, 978-1577316190

_____, *The Type Z Guide to Success: A Lazy Person's Manifesto to Wealth and Fulfillment*, 2006, 160p, New World Library, 978-1577315407

Ash, Mary Kay, *Timeless Principles from America's Greatest Woman Entrepreneur*, 2008, 272p, Wiley, 978-0470379950

Bach, David, *The Automatic Millionaire: A Powerful One-Step Plan to Live and Finish Rich*, 2005, 272p, Broadway, 978-0767923828

Barron, David R. & Danek S. Kaus, *Power Persuasion: Using Hypnotic Influence to Win in Life, Love, and Business*, 2005, 108p, Robert D. Reed Publishers, 978-1931741521

Bauer, Joel et al., *How to Persuade People Who Don't Want to Be Persuaded: Get What You Want Every Time!*, 2004, 256p, Wiley, 978-0471647973

Bedell, Gene, *Three Steps to Yes: The Gentle Art of Getting Your Way*, 2002, 256p, Three Rivers Press, 978-0609807194

Ben-Shahar, Tal, *Happier: Learn the Secrets to Daily Joy and Lasting Fulfillment*, 2007, 224p, McGraw-Hill, 978-0071492393

Bettger, Fred, *How I Raised Myself from Failure to Success in Selling*, 1992, 192p, Fireside; 978-0671794378

Blanchard, Ken, & Sheldon Bowles, *Raving Fans: A Revolutionary Approach To Customer Service,* 1993, 160p, William Morrow, 978-0688123161

Bloom, Linda & Charlie, *101 Things I Wish I Knew When I Got Married: Simple Lessons to Make Love Last*, 2004, 256p, New World Library, 978-1577314240

Bowles, Sheldon, *see* Blanchard, Ken, & Sheldon Bowles

Byrne, Rhonda, *The Secret*, 2006, 198p, Atria Books, 978-1582701707

Campbell, Joseph, *The Hero with a Thousand Faces* (Bollingen Series, No. 17), 1972, 464p, Princeton University Press, 978-0691017846

Canfield, Jack & Mark Victor Hansen, *Chicken Soup for the Soul,* 2001, 480p, HCI, 978-1558749207

Carlson, Kristine, *Don't Sweat the Small Stuff for Women: Simple and Practical Ways to Do What Matters Most and Find Time for You*, 2001, 288p, Hyperion, 978-0786886029

Carlson, Richard, *Don't Sweat the Small Stuff – And It's All Small Stuff,* 1996, 272p, Hyperion, 978-0786881857

Chapman, Dr. Gary, *The Five Love Languages: How to Express Heartfelt Commitment to Your Mate*, 1995, 204p, Northfield Publishing , 978-1881273158

Churchill, Winston, *Never Give In!: The Best of Winston Churchill's Speeches*, 2004, 558p, Hyperion, 0786888709

Cialdini, Robert, *Influence: The Psychology of Persuasion* (Collins Business Essentials), 2006, 336p, Collins Business, 978-0061241895

Cohen, Alan, *Relax Into Wealth: How to Get More by Doing Less*, 2006, 240p, Tarcher, 978-1585425631

Collier, Robert, *The Secret of the Ages*, 2008, 164p, Wilder Publications, 978-1604591880

Confucius, *The Analects* (Oxford World's Classics), translated by Raymond Dawson, 2008, 160p, Oxford University Press, 978-0199540617

Covey, Stephen, *The 7 Habits of Highly Effective People*, 2004, 4p, FreePress, 978-0743269513

Cutler, Howard C., *see* Dalai Lama, The, & Howard C. Cutler

da Vinci, Leonardo & Serge Bramly, *Leonardo: The Artist and the Man*, (Illustrated), 1995, 512p, Penguin, 978-0140231755

Dahlkoetter, Dr. JoAnn, *Your Performing Edge: The Total Mind-body Program for Excellence in Sports, Business and Life*, 4th Ed., 2007, 264p, Pulgas Ridge Press, 978-0970407986

Dalai Lama, The, & Howard C. Cutler, *The Art of Happiness: A Handbook for Living*, 1998, 336p, Riverhead, 978-1573221115

DeNoon, Daniel, "Health-Food-Store Safari," WebMD.com

Disney, Walt, *Quotable Walt Disney*, 2001, 272p, Disney Editions, 978-0786853328

Dyer, Dr. Wayne, *Inspiration: Your Ultimate Calling*, 2007, 272p, Hay House, 978-1401907228

_____, *Your Erroneous Zones*, 1993, 320p, Avon Books, 978-0061091483

Einstein, Albert, *The World As I See It*, 2006, 128p, Filiquarian Publishing , 978-1599869650

Emerson, Ralph Waldo, *Emerson: Essays and Lectures: Nature: Addresses and Lectures / Essays: First and Second Series / Representative Men / English Traits / The Conduct of Life*, 1983, 1150p, Library of America, 978-0940450158

Fettke, Rich, *Extreme Success: The 7-Part Program That Shows You How to Succeed Without Struggle*, 2002, 288p, Fireside, 978-0743223140

Franklin, Benjamin, *Benjamin Franklin: Autobiography, Poor Richard, and Later Writings* (Library of America), J. A. Leo Lemay ed., 2005, 816p, Library of America, 978-1883011536

Gage, Randy, *Why You're Dumb, Sick & Broke ... And How to Get Smart, Healthy & Rich!*, 2006, 224p, Wiley, 978-0470049310

Gandhi, Mahatma, *An Autobiography: The Story of My Experiments With Truth*, 1993, 528p, Beacon Press, 978-0807059098

Gilbert, Bill *see* King, Larry & Bill Gilbert

Gospe, Mike, *Marketing Campaign Development: What Marketing Executives Need to Know About Architecting Global Integrated Marketing Campaigns*, 2008, 176p, Happy About, 978-1600050770

Greene, Bob, *Get with the Program!: Getting Real About Your Weight, Health, and Emotional Well-Being*, 2003, 224p, Simon & Schuster Australia, 978-0731811892

Groppel, Jack L., PhD, *The Anti-Diet Book*, 1995

Hansen, Mark Victor *see* Canfield, Jack & Mark Victor Hansen

Hayden, C. J., *Get Clients Now!*, 2nd Ed., 2007, 256p, AMACOM, 978-0814473740

Hendricks, Gay, *The Big Leap: Conquer Your Hidden Fear and Take Life to the Next Level*, 2009, 224p, HarperOne, 978-0061735349

Hepburn, Katherine, *Me: Stories of My Life*, 1996, 432p, Ballantine Books, 978-0345410092

Jampolsky, Gerald "Jerry," MD, *Love is Letting Go of Fear*, 25th Anniversary Ed., 2004, 144p, Ten Speed Press, 978-1587611964

Jay, Robin, *The Art of the Business Lunch: Building Relationships Between 12 and 2*, 2006, 254p, Career Press, 978-1564148513

Jung, Carl, *The Portable Carl Jung* (Viking Portable Library), Joseph Campbell ed.,1976, 704p, Penguin, 978-014015070

Kaus, Danek S. *see* Barron, David R. + Danek S. Kaus

Kaus, Danek S., *You Can Be Famous: Insider Secrets to Getting Free Publicity*, 2009, 176p, Robert Reed Publishers, 978-1934759110

Kawasaki, Guy, *The Art of the Start: The Time-Tested, Battle-Hardened Guide for Anyone Starting Anything*, 2004, 226p, Portfolio Hardcover, 978-1591840565

Keller, Helen, *The Story of My Life: The Restored Classic*, Centennial Ed., Anne Sullivan et al. eds, 2003, 352p, W. W. Norton & Company, 978-0393057447

Kennedy, John F., *Let the Word Go Forth: The Speeches, Statements, and Writings of John F. Kennedy 1947 to 1963*, Theodore Sorensen ed, 1991, 448p, Delta, 978-0440504061

King, Larry & Bill Gilbert, *How to Talk to Anyone, Anytime, Anywhere: The Secrets of Good Communication*, 1995, 224p, Three Rivers Press, 978-0517884539

King, Jr., Martin Luther, *A Testament of Hope: The Essential Writings and Speeches of Martin Luther King, Jr.*, James M. Washington ed., 1990, 736p, HarperOne, 978-0060646912

Kiyosaki, Robert T. & Sharon L. Lechter, *Rich Dad, Poor Dad: What the Rich Teach Their Kids About Money – That the Poor and Middle Class Do Not!*, 2000, 207p, Business Plus, 978-0446677455

Klein, MA, CSP, Allen, *The Healing Power of Humor*, 1989, 240p, Tarcher, 978-0874775198

Kushner, Malcolm, *Presentations for Dummies*, 2004, 384p, For Dummies, 978-0764559556

_____, *Public Speaking for Dummies*, 2nd Ed., 2004, 288p, For Dummies; 978-0764559549

Lao-Tzu, *Te-Tao Ching – A New Translation Based on the Recently Discovered Ma-wang-tui Texts* (Classics of Ancient China), tranlated by Robert G. Henricks, 1992, 430p, Ballantine Books, 978-0345370990

Lee, Michael Soon, MBA & Sensei Grant Tabuchi, *Black Belt Negotiating: Become a Master Negotiator Using Powerful Lessons from the Martial Arts*, 2007, 224p, Amacom Books, 978-0814474617

Lee, Michael Soon, Ralph R. Roberts, & Joe Kraynak, *Cross-Cultural Selling for Dummies*, (Illustrated), 2008, 384p, For Dummies, 0470377011

Levinson, Jay Conrad, *Guerrilla Marketing: Easy and Inexpensive Strategies for Making Big Profits from Your Small Business*, 4th Ed., 2007, 384p, Mariner Books , 978-0618785919

Luskin, Dr. Fred, *Forgive for Good*, 2003, 240p, HarperOne, 978-0062517210

Luskin, Dr. Fred, *Forgive for Love: The Missing Ingredient for a Healthy and Lasting Relationship*, 2009, 240p, HarperOne, 978-0061234958

MacFarlane, Michael, *Share and Grow Rich: The Dottie Walters Effect*, 2007, 207p, Elevate, 978-1601940087

Marcoux, Tom, *10 Best Kept Secrets of Persuasion Masters*, Marcoux Media

_____, *101 Acting Secrets: Tips from A Director for Your Acting, Auditions, Movie Roles, and Self-Promotion*, Marcoux Media, www.TomSuperCoach.com

_____, *Be Heard and Be Trusted: How You Can Use Secrets of the Greatest Communicators to Get What You Want, 3rd Ed.*, 2009, Marcoux Media, 978-0-9800511-4-8

_____, *Darkest Secrets of Persuasion and Seduction Masters: How to Protect Yourself and Turn the Power to Good*, 2006, 186p, Marcoux Media, 978-0-9800511-0-0

_____, *Double Your Sales in Half the Time*, Marcoux Media

_____, *Empower Your Personal Brand: Align Yourself for Promotions and Raises*, Marcoux Media

_____, *How to Heal When Life's Too Much*, Marcoux Media

_____, *Make Money through Products Power*, Marcoux Media

_____, *Nothing Can Stop You This Year!: How to Unleash Your Hidden Power to Persuade Well, Get More Done, Gain Sudden Profits, Command Intuition, and Feel Great*, 2nd Ed., 2010, Tom Marcoux Media, 978-0-9800511-5-5

_____, *Online Secrets to Build Your Brand*, Marcoux Media

_____, *Personal Branding*, Marcoux Media

_____, *Power Time Management: More Time, Less Stress and Zero Procrastination*, Marcoux Media

_____, *Say Yes to Yourself: Secrets to Overcome Stress and Change in Your Workplace*, Marcoux Media

_____, *Secret Influence to Get You Out of Trouble: How You Can Restore a Personal or Business Relationship After You've Really Screwed Up*, 2008, 156p, Marcoux Media, 978-0-9800511-3-1, www.TomSuperCoach.com

_____, *The Recession-Proof Cupcake: How to Feed Your Soul, Save a Business, or Get a Job in a Crisis*, Marcoux Media

_____, *Truth No One Will One Tell You: How to Feed Your Soul, Save a Business, or Get a Job in a Crisis*, 2010, Tom Marcoux Media, 978-0-9800511-6-2

_____, *Ultimate Make Money While You Sleep via the Internet System*, Marcoux Media, www.TomSuperCoach.com

_____, *Wake Up Your Spirit to Prosperity for Couples!: 7 Secrets to Increase Wealth, Romance, and Anything You Want*, 2006, 150p, Marcoux Media, 0-9624660-6-9

_____, *Wake Up Your Spirit to Prosperity!: 7 Secrets to Attract Wealth, Love, and Anything You Want*, 2006, 132p, Marcoux Media, 0-9624660-5-0

McWilliams, Peter, *Wealth 101: Getting What You Want-Enjoying What You've Got*, 1999, 532p, Prelude Press, 978-0931580185

Melograni, Piero, *Wolfgang Amadeus Mozart: A Biography*, 2008, 316p, University Of Chicago Press, 978-0226519616

O'Connor, Michael J. *see* Alessandra, Dr. Tony & Michael J. O'Connor

Orman, Suze, *The Laws of Money: 5 Timeless Secrets to Get Out and Stay Out of Financial Trouble*, 2004, 352p, Free Press, 978-0743245180

Parnell, Aaron Lloyd U., *Living with Vitality – The Dynamic Power of Extraordinary Health*, 2007, 204p, PZQ Press Divison, 978-0615143323

Ragas, Matthew W. and B. J. Bueno, *The Power of Cult Branding: How 9 Magnetic Brands Turned Customers into Loyal Followers (and Yours Can, Too!)*, 2002, 224p, Crown Business, 978-0761536949

Reeve, Christopher, *Nothing is Impossible: Reflections on a New Life*, 2004, 224p, Ballantine Books, 978-0345470737

RoAnne, Susan, *How to Work a Room*, Revised Ed., 2007, 336p, Collins Living, 978-0061238673

Robbins, Anthony, *Awaken the Giant Within: How to Take Immediate Control of Your Mental, Emotional, Physical and Financial Destiny!*, 1992, 544p, Free Press, 978-0671791544

Robbins, Mike, CSP, *Be Yourself, Everyone Else is Already Taken: Transform Your Life with the Power of Authenticity*, 2009, 256p, Jossey-Bass, 978-0470395011

_____, *Focus on the Good Stuff: The Power of Appreciation*, 2007, 240p, Jossey-Bass, 978-0787988791

Roffer, Robin Fisher, *Make a Name for Yourself: Eight Steps Every Woman Needs to Create a Personal Brand Strategy for Success*, 2002, 224p, Broadway, 978-0767904926

Savage, PhD, Elayne, *Don't Take It Personally! The Art of Dealing with Rejection*, 2002, 242p, iUniverse, 978-0595255757

_____, *Breathing Room – Creating Space to Be a Couple*, 2001, 210p, New Harbinger Publications, 978-1572242210

Seid, Syndi, *Etiquette in Minutes*, www.etiquetteinminutes.com

Siddhartha, Guatama, *In the Buddha's Words: An Anthology of Discourses from the Pali Canon* (Teachings of the Buddha), Bhikkhu Bodhi ed., 2005, 496p, Wisdom Publications, 978-0861714919

Siegel, Dr. Bernie, *Love, Medicine and Miracles: Lessons Learned about Self-Healing from a Surgeon's Experience with Exceptional Patients*, 1990, 256p, Harper, 978-0060919832

Spielberg, Steven, *Interviews* (Conversations with Filmmakers Series), Lester D. Friedman & Brent Notbohm eds., 2000, 250p, University Press of Mississippi, 978-1578061136

St. John, Noah, *The Secret Code of Success*, 2009, 256p, Collins Business, 978-0061715747

Tabuchi, Sensei Grant *see* Lee, Michael Soon, MBA & Sensei Grant Tabuchi

Teresa, Mother, *Mother Teresa: In My Own Words*, edited by Jose Luis Gonzalez-Balado, 1997, 128p, Liguori Publications, 978-0764802003

Tracy, Brian, *Eat That Frog!: 21 Great Ways to Stop Procrastinating and Get More Done in Less Time*, 2nd Ed., 2007, 128p, Berrett-Koehler Publishers, 978-1576754221

Trump, Donald J., *The Art of the Deal*, 2004, 384p, Ballantine Books, 978-0345479174

Waitley, Denis, *The Psychology of Winning*, 1987, Nightingale-Conant, 0671520679, audio recording (also available in paperback)

Walters, Dottie & Lillet "Lilly" Walters, *Speak and Grow Rich*, 1997, 288p, Prentice Hall, 978-0735203518

Wattles, Wallace D., *The Science of Getting Rich*, 2008, 112p, Wilder Publications, 978-1604591903

Wieder, Marcia, *Making Your Dreams Come True*, 1999, 235p, Harmony, 978-0609606087

Williams, A.L., *All You Can Do Is All You Can Do, But All You Can Do Is Enough!*, 1997, 219p, Ballantne Books, 978-0449001103

Winfrey, Oprah & O, The Oprah Magazine, Editors of O, *Live Your Best Life: A Treasury of Wisdom, Wit, Advice, Interviews, and Inspiration from O, The Oprah Magazine*, 2005, 336p, Oxmoor House, 978-0848731052

_____ & Bill Adler, *The Uncommon Wisdom Of Oprah Winfrey: A Portrait in Her Own Words*, 2000, 290p, Citadel, 978-1559724197

Ziglar, Zig, *Goals – Set goals ... and reach them!*, 1988, Nightingale-Conant, audio recording

Index

D

E

L

M

Marcoux, Tom – i, iii, iv, v, 3, 68,
153, 178, 214, 237, 251, 259,
262, 281, 285, 291, 293,
328–329, 349–351, 354
Marcus – 52
Marina – 100, 101, 102, 103
Markova, Dawna – 69
Marta – 145
Martha – 15
Mary Kay Cosmetics – 134, 213
Massachusset Institute of
Technology – 128
mastermind group – 74, 75, 308
Matsushita, Konosuke – 136
Matt – 247
Maugham, Somerset – 69
Max Planck Institute for Human
Development – 3
Maya – 6
Mayo Clinic – 47, 50, 54
McAvoy, Esme – 282
McQuarie, Ralph – 217
McWilliams, Peter – 329
meditation – 117, 282, 284, 288, 307
meeting – 63, 74, 75, 159, 160, 162,
163, 164, 166, 170, 182, 186,
251, 259
Mei – 16
Melograni, Piero – 329
memes – 273, 303
memorable phrase – 155, 156, 157,
210, 212, 299
memory, group – 162, 170
metaphor – 269, 270, 271, 273, 274,
303

metaphor, global – 266, 270, 271,
273, 274, 303, 307
"me, too" identifying – 146
Microsoft – 85, 86
Milestones Binder – 13, 62, 63, 73,
300, 308
Miller, David C. – 123
Miller, Henry – 232
mindset – 11, 246
Mira – 31
Mission Caption – iii, 30, 31, 308
MIT ➠ Massachussets Institute of
Technology
money – 4, 9, 10, 16, 86, 90, 91, 118,
124, 137, 139, 142, 147, 154, 171,
195, 205, 232, 272, 278, 311
money, trading time for – 139, 142
mood – 19, 26, 47, 48, 57, 76, 81, 82,
84, 85, 91, 101, 121, 125, 128,
256, 276, 284, 298
Mozart, Wolfgang Amadeus – 329

N

Nadine – 101
Naisbitt, John – 134
Nardi, Bonnie – 171
National Assoc. of Broadcasters
Conference – 10, 350
National Speakers Association – 350
negativity – 82, 83, 103, 251, 255,
258, 262, 266, 267, 274, 281,
288, 313
Nerburn, Kent – 275
networking – 34, 186, 210, 211
Nina – 199

R

S

About the Author

Tom Marcoux
America's Communication Coach

Tom Marcoux helps people like *you* accomplish big dreams. As Tom says, "I help people like you *command the Wow!* in your audience. When presenting, branding, or communicating one-on-one, my coaching helps you make people feel good and *want* to follow your lead." Further, Tom helps people get more done and feel good doing it.

Tom is also a prolific author, including *Truth No One Will You*, he has published 10 books and 21 audio programs, with sales in 15 countries. These have included both fiction and nonfiction. Prominent among his publications is *Be Heard & Be Trusted*, 3rd Ed., which, in a prior edition, was a required textbook at Cogswell Polytechnical College. The Third edition features contributions by Jay Conrad Levinson, Guy Kawasaki, and Dr. Fred Luskin, among others.

When you want *to influence others*, join Tom's many clients who benefit from his secrets on branding. Tom is described as "the Personal Branding Instructor" by the *San*

Francisco Examiner. Helping people become more effective job candidates, he has presented to ProMatch, Project Management Institute and chapters of Experience Unlimited (affiliated with the California Employment Development Department).

Holding a degree in psychology, Tom is also a personal and professional coach and guest expert on TV and radio. In addition to being featured in technology and communication magazines, he earned a special award at the Emmy Awards. For six years, he addressed the National Association of Broadcasters Conference in Las Vegas on topics like, "Online Secrets to Build Your Brand."

Tom is an award-winning speaker and corporate workshop leader (to professionals from IBM, Wells Fargo, Sun Microsystems, and Silicon Valley Bank). He is a member of the National Speakers Association.

Tom is also a faculty lecturer in public speaking, science fiction and fantasy literature and cinema, and comparative religion at Academy of Art University. He has been a guest lecturer at Stanford University, DeAnza College, and California State University at Los Angeles, among others. In addition to traditional classroom forums, he teaches online and has authored several online courses. He also presents workshops to fellow faculty at the Academy of Art University's Teacher Conferences.

In a more artistic vein, Tom has written, directed, and produced feature films, including one that went to the Cannes Film Festival market, where it gained international distribution. He performed as an actor in feature films and commercials. Presently, he is leading teams working on book-film projects titled *Crystal Pegasus* (children's fantasy) and *TimePulse* (science fiction). In addition, his audio programs and audio novels often feature orginal soundtracks composed by Tom.

When you need to enthrall audiences or effectively communicate your message to the media, engage Tom as your media coach. Tom will clarify your message, build your confidence in speaking, and craft compelling sound bites and stories for the press. Tom will help you excel!

(415) 572-6609
TomSuperCoach@gmail.com
www.TomSuperCoach.com

Designed

and set by gBambo of the graphic
and cartographic atelier:

kunst**+aventur**

Named for the slim booklet *Kunst
und Aventur* (Art & Enterprise),
published in Strasbourg, France in
1440, in which Johannes Gutenberg
(*c.* 1398 – 1468), a German goldsmith,
unveiled his epochal mechanization
of printing, vastly accelerating   the
pace of learning and human progress.

The text was set principally in Minion
Pro, Zapf Humanist, Poor Richard,
Fontin, and Gill Sans families. The
body font, Minion Pro, was designed
by Robert Slimbach based on classical
old style types of the late Renaissance.

The design was executed in Adobe's
excellent Creative Suite 4, including
Photoshop, Illustrator, and InDesign.

Photographic kit was a Nikon D70
DSLR fitted with a Nikkor ED AF-S
24-120mm 1.3-5.6 G VR lens.

Write kunst.aventur@gmail.com
about design inquiries large or small
and user feedback.
Enjoy!

Collophon

Get what you really want ...

use the methods found in Tom Marcoux's books!

For special discounts, order at:
www.TomSuperCoach.com/SpecialOffer.htm

Nothing Can Stop You This Year!

Be Heard & Be Trusted — How You Can Use the Secrets of...

Wake Up Your Spirit to Prosperity for Couples! — 7 Secrets to increase wealth, romance, and awaken true trust — Tom Marcoux

WAKE UP YOUR SPIRIT TO PROSPERITY! — 7 secrets to attract wealth, love, and anything you want — Tom Marcoux

SECRET INFLUENCE TO GET YOU OUT OF TROUBLE — Tom Marcoux

Truth No One Will Tell You — Tom Marcoux

DARKEST SECRETS of Persuasion and Seduction Masters — How to Protect Yourself and Turn the Power to Good — Tom Marcoux

For more QuickBreakthrough resources, see
www.TomSuperCoach.com

www.ingramcontent.com/pod-product-compliance
Lightning Source LLC
Chambersburg PA
CBHW071403090426
42737CB00011B/1334